WARRIOR PUPS

WARRIOR PUPS

PUPS | TRUE STORIES OF AMERICA'S K9 HEROES

★ ★ ★ ★ ★ ★ ★ **JEFF KAMEN** ★ ★ ★ ★ ★ ★ ★

WITH LESLIE STONE-KAMEN

Guilford, Connecticut

An imprint of Globe Pequot

Distributed by NATIONAL BOOK NETWORK

British Library Cataloguing in Publication Information Available

Library of Congress Cataloging-in-Publication Data

Names: Kamen, Jeff, author. | Stone-Kamen, Leslie, author. | Deltuva, Janet, photographer.
Title: Warrior pups : true stories of America's K9 heroes / Jeff Kamen with Leslie Stone-Kamen ;
    with photos by Janet Deltuva.
Other titles: True stories of America's K9 heroes
Description: Guilford, Connecticut : Lyons Press, [2017]
Identifiers: LCCN 2017009950 (print) | LCCN 2017012812 (ebook) | ISBN 9781493029662 (ebook) |
    ISBN 9781493029655 (hardcover)
Subjects: LCSH: Dogs—War use—United States. | Belgian malinois—United States. | Lackland Air Force
    Base (Tex.)
Classification: LCC UH100 (ebook) | LCC UH100 .K57 2017 (print) | DDC
    355.4/240929—dc23
LC record available at https://lccn.loc.gov/2017009950

♾™ The paper used in this publication meets the minimum requirements of American National Standard for Information Sciences—Permanence of Paper for Printed Library Materials, ANSI/NISO Z39.48-1992.

Printed in the United States of America

To America's Military Working Dog teams whose love, bravery, and training protect our troops.

To the patriotic men and women—civilian and military—who volunteer as fosters to raise our homegrown baby warrior pups.

To the 341st Training Squadron at Joint Base San Antonio-Lackland Air Force Base, whose staff breeds, acquires, and provides basic training for the dogs and their heroic human handlers.

To the team at Holland Memorial Hospital for Military Working Dogs and the Lackland Kennel caretakers.

To Chief Bob Rubio who opened the doors.

To the great public champions of America's Military Working Dogs who have been with them in battle and went on to advocate their cause in Congress and in the press, including John Burnam, James Harrington, Chris Willingham, and Ron Aiello, founder of the United States War Dogs Association.

To our editor Holly Rubino at Lyons Press who conceptualized this book and guided us with a sure hand and a joyful spirit.

To Maria Goodavage, whose popular books opened the minds and hearts of Americans to our inspiring working dogs and, though on deadline herself, took the time to encourage me as I wrote.

To Professor Peter Laufer at the University of Oregon and The Swan who always keep the faith.

To my children, Nathan, Morley, Sydney, and Gavi, whose deep love of and respect for dogs always made me proud.

To Zog, Yukon, Kodiak, Argus, and Blue who always had our backs as well as our hearts. We'll see you on the other side of The Rainbow Bridge.

SERVICE AND SACRIFICE:
COUNTLESS THOUSANDS OF
AMERICAN SERVICEMEN'S CHILDREN,
GRANDCHILDREN, AND GREAT GRANDCHILDREN
WERE BORN BECAUSE AMERICA GAVE HER
SONS AND DAUGHTERS A DOG TO SAVE LIVES
IN TIME OF WAR. PART OF THE
FOR AMERICA'S FREEDOM AND
BELONGS TO THE MILITARY WORKING DOGS
WHO SERVE ON THE BATTLEFIELD ALONGSIDE
THEIR FAITHFUL MASTERS. TOGETHER THEY
BOTH STRIVE VALIANTLY, AS A TEAM, TO
BRAVELY DEFEND THEIR GROUND, BECAUSE
THEY KNOW THAT DECISIVE VICTORY IS SAVING
AMERICAN LIVES. AND WHEN DEATH TAKES HIS
MASTER ON THE BATTLEFIELD, THERE HIS DOG
WILL BE FOUND, HIS EYES SAD BUT VIGILANT,
FAITHFUL AND TRUE TO THE VERY END.
"IF THERE ARE NO DOGS IN HEAVEN, THEN
WHEN I DIE I WANT TO GO WHERE THEY WENT."
—WILL ROGERS
LERS AND THEIR BELOVED
ENEMY, AND SAVE LIVES

CONTENTS

PHOTOS BY JANET DELTUVA.

INTRODUCTION

Dogs, family, God, country, and storytelling are the great passions of my life. I've always been especially inspired by the lives of America's Military Working Dogs (MWDs) and their heroic handlers. So, when I was asked to write the book now in your hands, it was the dream assignment of a long journalism career that has taken me around the world. It took months to negotiate our way into Lackland, the US Air Force base whose inspiring K9 team raises and trains almost all of America's Military Working Dogs. But in the end, the Air Force welcomed my photojournalist wife Leslie and me. We were given a full month to go everywhere and talk to everyone with no governmental effort to spin or otherwise control what we saw. They didn't need to. Lackland turns out to be a jewel in the crown of US military achievement. There are more than two thousand MWDs deployed around the world. Almost all of them started at this one base in south Texas. Warrior pups with names that have double first letters like WWick, SSharif, PPatriot, and PPershing were born at Lackland and account for about 20 percent of our military K9s. The other 80 percent are purchased at about 13 months old from dog brokers in Europe. The US Defense Department pays more than four thousand dollars per pup. No matter where they are born, they all get their basic training at the Dog Training School inside Lackland.

Fosters with their new puppies. PHOTO COURTESY LACKLAND FOSTER COMMUNITY.

These pups were bred by the Defense Department to protect American troops. First, they have to be raised by loving volunteer civilian and military foster families. PHOTO BY JANET DELTUVA.

Dog Training School and Handlers' Course instructors begin their day with Guard Mount staff meetings in the building behind this fighter plane from a bygone era. PHOTO BY JEFF KAMEN.

Once we were allowed on the base, we dug into the Defense Department's Military Working Dog Breeding Program (also known as the Breeding Program and the Puppy Program), the Puppy School, the Dog Training School, the Handlers' Course, and the vast kennels system of Lackland K9. All those elements are supported by the superb staff of Holland Memorial Hospital for Military Working Dogs—the only one of its kind in America. Wherever we went at Lackland, we had a great time.

As you turn the following pages, you will meet warrior pups and the people who transform them into war dogs. First, we introduce you to the maternity ward, then to some of the inspiring foster families who raise the puppies. Then, it's back inside Lackland to the Puppy School, the Dog Training School, the Handlers' Course, the kennels, and Holland Hospital. We'll also be taking you from Lackland into the field—from Alaska to the Middle East—to gain insights into the lives of our Military Working Dog (MWD) teams. You will encounter the greatest living American Military Working Dog, who survived a devastating bombing to enjoy his retirement, and you will also witness the precious last hours of another Military Working Dog—one who lost his fight to cancer.

These are stories of great love, patriotism, and dedication. It all begins in a space that most people will never be allowed to enter. It's where carefully selected war dogs are bred, where their puppies are born, and where the natural bond between military canines and their human handlers is first nurtured. Only properly trained Military Working Dog teams can reliably safeguard our troops from the hidden threats of IEDs (Improvised Explosive Devices) and terrorist ambushes. The sincere dedication of our military to these dogs comes, in part, from the understanding that on average, each American war dog saves 150 human lives during the dog's career.

Leslie and I were fortunate to stay in the home of an Air Force enlisted couple and their three Belgian Malinois dogs in rural Devine, Texas, a thirty-five-minute drive from Lackland. When they are not on duty, these two patriots who have fostered nine pups, host a closed Facebook page for hundreds of San Antonio area families. Thanks to "The Musicians" (see their chapter) we got to share in the lives of many fosters. We listened to their stories, played with their dogs, and enjoyed their killer Texas chili and cornbread.

Raising these pups is a lot more demanding than bringing up a typical house dog because of all the requirements for exercise and socialization. Also, if you become a foster, you are shouldering some of the responsibility for protecting our fighting men and women. As one trainer told me privately, "Great foster, great dog! Not-so-great foster, lots more work for us trainers."

Mike, the mustached man holding the puppy in the front row of the photo on page ix, has raised many warrior pups for the Breeding Program. He told me that what he and other fosters do is selfless service to the nation. "We're volunteers and we know that when the sweet puppy we've fallen in love with reaches adolescence at seven months, we've got to return him to Lackland where he will begin formal training. We also know that we may never see him again. It's emotionally tough, but it is so worth it!"

Within minutes of our first arrival at Lackland, a senior noncommissioned officer (NCO) gave Leslie and me these orders: "Wherever you go, whatever you are observing, don't get closer to the dogs than fifteen feet!" We followed the NCO from the Lackland Visitor Center down winding roads, out of the base, across a public road, and into another secure area. It's called the Medina Annex and it's huge. Soon, we were off pavement, bouncing in our SUV behind the Air Force truck driven by our guide. The truck came to a stop in the middle of a rough field. There the NCO climbed down from the truck and told us, "This training area is called 'The Pit.' When you are here observing the dogs as they learn to search for bombs and drugs and do patrol work, keep

I take a bite from Military Working Dog Anna during a training exercise. Without that bite sleeve I would have needed a hospital. PHOTO BY LESLIE STONE-KAMEN.

in mind that this is wild land with real rattlesnakes, real fire ants, and real wild boar. So please stay aware of your surroundings. You start at the Air Force's 341st Training Squadron, Dog Training School. Guard Mount is at 0600 sharp, third floor, the building with the big 37 on it and the cool fighter plane with the shark face in front. Got it? Good."

As he climbed back into his truck, Leslie looked around The Pit and declared, "Let's get out of here before the snakes and the wild boar come looking for new friends!"

For a solid month, we were privileged insiders at Lackland K9. We learned that the people who make it all happen are smart, brave, passionate, funny, and human—so they watch out for each other's mistakes to guarantee the success of their mission. This absolutely vital work demands everything you've got every day and that pushes the envelope for everyone. "We don't employ any super-heroes here," says one Red Patch Master Trainer, whom you will soon meet, as he carefully risks his own safety to help a very strong dog with large teeth learn to trust.

Since we began our story-gathering at Lackland, we've been honored to become part of the global American military K9 community. We've made friends for life and been granted the privilege of sharing in the adventure that goes on every day inside Lackland. Now, it's your turn. 🐾

AUTHOR'S NOTE

A famed American anti-terrorist told me privately, "Protect their identities," regarding the members of the Lackland K9 community to reduce the risk of making them targets for terrorists, so we use their real first names and last initials only throughout. Those who are stationed elsewhere might return to Lackland, so their identities are also protected. 🐾

Dog Training School instructor T. Sgt. James M. wears half a bite protection suit after a K9 demonstration inside Lackland. That's his family. PHOTO BY JEFF KAMEN.

CHAPTER 1

MEET THE NEWBORNS

This is where it all begins: the cradle of the Military Working Dog Breeding Program for the entire Defense Department. Hundreds of US war dogs who are on duty around the world right now started life right here in this small building at Lackland Air Force Base in San Antonio.

Every year in the squeaky clean, meticulously climate-controlled K9 maternity ward (technically referred to as the "Whelping Kennel") about one hundred new puppies are born. Their parents are from long lines of bold, smart Belgian Malinois herding dogs with powerful hunting drives, which make them ideal as war dogs. By the time the puppies are six weeks old, they are off their mother's milk and start eating an expensive, government-supplied prescription diet.

Each new puppy commands the complete attention of the whelping staff and vet techs assigned to them. Most of the puppies in the same litter may look similar, but within days of their birth, their individual personalities begin to emerge.

Whelping Kennel and Breeding Program staffers get to enjoy forty-two days with these canine babies before they are placed with volunteer military and civilian foster families who raise them over the following five and a half months. During that time, the puppies develop physically, psychologically, and socially at a rapid rate.

Instructors at the Dog Training School say Breeding Program dogs are often easier to train than imported dogs because of the way our warrior pups have been handled from the very beginning of their lives in the whelping kennel, in foster care, and then at Puppy School. The first year is a key formative time for any dog, but especially important for future Military Working Dogs.

Each newborn warrior pup at Lackland is not only nurtured and adored, but closely monitored. All of this is the result of the finely tuned breeding process directed by Dr. Stewart H. (better known as "Doc"), the acclaimed manager of the Military Working Dog Breeding Program.

In about two years, these sweet little puppies will be capable of detecting and taking down threats to our troops. PHOTO BY LINDA HOSEK.

BREED OF CHOICE

Belgian Malinois dogs are more rugged than other power breeds, have fewer medical problems (such as the hip dysplasia that afflicts so many German shepherds), and weigh less than most shepherds by ten pounds or more. That can mean a lot if you have to carry your hurt dog on your back for miles or if you need to get in or out of a tight space, like a helicopter, fast.

"We choose breeding dogs with great care. We look for working dog parents who show high levels of environmental boldness." says Doc. "It is important that the dogs not be easily frightened, even when people are shooting at them or trying to blow them up along with the troops they protect," and that, says Doc, should mean they're going to make good working dogs. But that is not the only challenge these canines must face. "Dogs who are bold and unaffected in acutely stressful environments like combat will also do well with the less dramatic, but long-term stressors that practically all Military Working Dogs must deal with," says Doc. These are the same stressors that human warriors must routinely endure, and according to Doc, "That includes lack of privacy and down-time, overcrowding, fear and tension, sensory overload, dislocation while abruptly transitioning from one unfamiliar environment to another, long periods of soul-killing boredom, and tremendous psychological pressure while actually on the job." Doc explains all this between training sessions.

The Lackland kennels are run with love by a dedicated team, but Doc points out that his Breeding Program puppies go from the sweet space of the maternity unit to the adoring arms of foster parents who usually treat them as special house pets. "Then, at the half-grown age of seven months," says Doc, "they are suddenly taken away from the people and places they know and deposited into this large kennel, where they are very well cared for but it's definitely not the comforts of their previous home."

Think of their life in the kennels and the various levels of training, says Doc, as analogous to military training for aspiring human warriors—the young men and women who make the serious commitment to enlist in our armed services. "This basic training experience is the crucible that either tempers the hard metal in those individuals meant to be warrior dogs and human

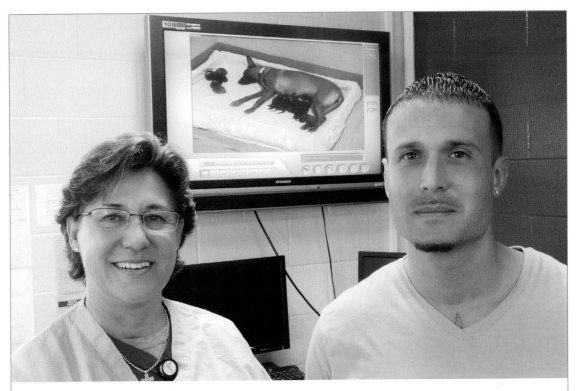

Whelping Kennel staffers Solange L. and Kyle M. with a mother dog and her babies on the live video monitor.
PHOTO BY JEFF KAMEN.

beings, or it shows them to be better fitted for another life not devoted to the profession of arms," Doc says.

"In the kennels, once they are seven months old, some puppies quickly lose their hard edge of confidence and self-assurance and their vital drive to do work, and as a result, those pups respond poorly once they enter training." These unhappy young dogs, says Doc, "find themselves rather quickly re-deposited back in their foster homes among the cushions and kisses they prefer, while others rise to the challenges, gain confidence and power, and go on to thrive in training."

At one of his regular monthly sessions with fosters at which coffee and doughnuts abound and short informal training is done, Doc implores the volunteers who raise our future four-legged war fighters to avoid pampering them.

This newborn's eyes have just opened. DEFENSE DEPARTMENT PHOTO.

TOUGH STUFF

The earliest evaluation of the puppies' suitability as American Military Working Dogs begins within a matter of days after their birth. How they play and respond to people are all good indicators. Two years after their birth in the Lackland K9 maternity ward, some of these puppies will be fully certified in patrol and detection and ready for the advanced training that leads to being deployed into harm's way.

One of the fosters, Sarah K., shoots back, "But they're my babies!"

The room bursts into laughter and Doc playfully retorts, "See! That's what I'm talking about!"

But everyone in the foster community knows that Sarah also has one of the highest success rates. Most of the dogs she fosters go on to graduate the Dog Training School and are now safeguarding our troops. Doc loves her results while being skeptical about her approach.

Doc is one of the most knowledgeable people in the world on raising and training Military Working Dogs, but he is frustrated by what he still does not know. "Even though you have eminent people in our military and political life saying they know that there's no better countermeasure against the threats that we face than a high-quality, well-trained dog, there is still so much we do not know about these powerful animals because of the inadequate amount of research dollars," he says. "We need to spend more to increase our understanding of them, increase our understanding of how to better breed them, how to more effectively rear them, train them, and how to better deploy them. The

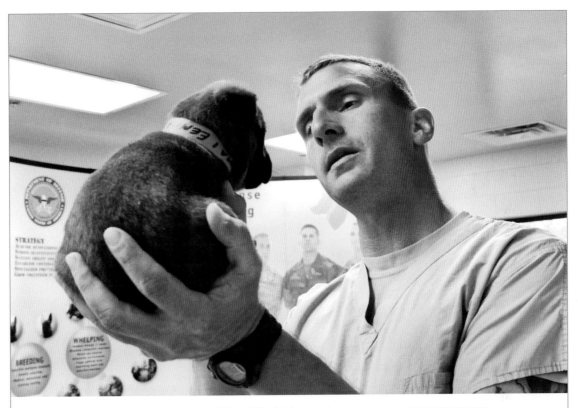

Fierce or fearful? Some litters produce both kinds. Why this happens is a mystery. DEFENSE DEPARTMENT PHOTO.

amount of research dollars that are spent on this are not nearly commensurate with the importance of these dogs."

Meanwhile, another litter of potential K9 heroes is about to be born at Lackland. Some of these puppies will "make a dog," which is what the trainers call a warrior pup who passes all its tests, while others from the very same litter will wash out of the program but go on to have enjoyable lives of service—just not in the military. 🐾

CHAPTER 2

HEALER OF BROKEN HEARTS

When they decided to help their country, Laurel B. and her family got so much in return. Laurel, a software consultant in San Antonio, Texas, remembers how her family's fostering adventure with EEland began. "The day they handed me that handsome, warm puppy our family was still in mourning. We had suffered the death of our two dogs, one to old age and the other to an aggressive form of cancer. In just a few short months, we had gone from two dogs to none. Three weeks after our dog Hank died, I thought about reaching out to the DoD Breeding Program about fostering." Laurel, the mother of two girls, says, "It seemed perfect. We weren't ready to commit to a forever dog but something temporary, and with a purpose. In so many ways it seemed to be the remedy for a broken heart."

Laurel, her husband Rex B., and their two daughters were already huge fans of service dogs. They'd read quite a bit about MWDs, but weren't familiar with the Belgian Malinois breed. "We considered that we were fit for the fostering challenges due to our experiences with other big breed dogs," Laurel explains.

Puppy Program staffers hear this all the time. They smile politely and then wait for what they know is probably coming. They always brief the newbies on the energy and startling fierceness of Malinois puppies before they put the babies into the fosters' hands. But fosters, especially those who have previously raised German shepherds, rarely believe the warnings. The Puppy Program staffers often have to field phone calls from frantic fosters when they start to realize everything they've been told is true.

Three weeks after she applied to be a foster, Laurel's house and secure yard had been inspected and she was at Lackland for puppy orientation, surrounded by strangers, many in uniform. "I was out of my element from the minute I drove into Lackland. I had no direct military connection other than my father's service long before I was born."

Almost six months after this family took a puppy home to raise for the Breeding Program, it was time to give him back. PHOTO BY JANET DELTUVA.

Laurel was suddenly meeting people who spent their lives working inside a heavily guarded world that was devoted to keeping her and her family safe. San Antonio is home to tens of thousands of military personnel so she was used to seeing people in uniforms, but she had only driven by the base and had no idea what went on inside. That was then. Today, Lackland feels like home to her and her family.

"I had no idea so many of those people I met that first day would become such great friends to my family as we supported one another through the sometimes stormy periods of fostering," Laurel says. "In hindsight, it's funny. At orientation I heard about what to do if a dog bites, gets sick, or even if he eats a knife. The briefers were serious and I paid attention, so I was truly worried if we were up to all of this."

But something deep inside told her that she was doing the right thing for herself, for her family, and for her country. She hugged the puppy named EEland and drove him home with great care.

"When EEland arrived in our house," Laurel said, "our daughters immediately fell in love with him. My husband had been traveling on business. The moment he got home, the puppy recognized that Rex was his alpha and ran to his side. This was the new configuration of our family structure!"

This new foster family quickly came to embrace the detailed guidance given by the Puppy Program pros and the overarching message to fosters: Love the puppy and give him what he craves—the joy of being with humans. If that puppy ultimately does succeed, his entire life will be centered on the love of his handlers.

For EEland, his new life with Rex, Laurel, and their kids was immersion in a sea of endless kisses, hugs, and the more than seven hundred hours of play that is specifically prescribed in the Fostering Manual. That booklet, which is truly the bible for fosters, puts Doc H. inside the head of each of them, guiding them through the stages of Malinois puppy development. EEland thrived in his new home.

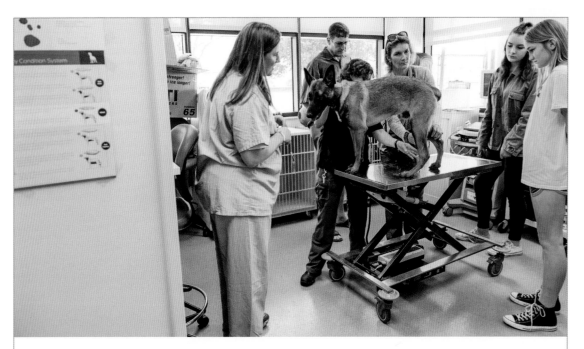

The foster pup receives his final health check at Holland Hospital before he leaves his loving foster family.
PHOTO BY JANET DELTUVA.

This pup turned out to have precisely what Doc was breeding for—very strong Belgian Malinois prey drive. Laurel quickly discovered that meant that everyone in the family had to be alert at all times. "EEland had to be on a leash when my daughters' friends were over so he wouldn't grab sleeves, pants, or skin! It was all play for him and he was getting bigger, stronger, and faster at every moment!"

EEland's roomy crate became a mainstay of the family's emerging coping strategies. EEland slept happily in the crate; this would be important for all the time he would spend in kennels and trailers as an MWD. They also put him in the crate when they needed a break from his unstoppable energy. "Actually, it was not until months into it that we realized we should have used that tactic more. He was exhausting, but we loved him," Laurel recalls with a wistful smile. There was a huge benefit to their devotion to a dog they knew they could not keep. "He became this wonderful, all-consuming project for our whole family. We didn't know it then but what a reward that was, to have all of us focusing on one important thing!"

Emotions intensified as the turn-in process was about to conclude. PHOTO BY JANET DELTUVA.

When he was out of his crate, the puppy engaged everything with his nose and teeth. "Baby EEland was canine chaos," Laurel laughs. "At the same time, he was the most loving little dog. He loved to snuggle. Following Doc's orders to socialize him, we took him everywhere we went so he could experience the world with all its noise and action." They went to the mall, the grocery store, even to an amusement park.

At the end of almost six months fostering EEland, Laurel had a new group of friends and "a dog that had burned his paw print into our hearts forever."

At age seven months, warrior pups must be turned in to the Breeding Program for the beginning of their formal training and life in the Lackland kennels. Some foster families refer to that time as the day their foster dog "reports for duty." For Laurel and her family, EEland's turn-in is engraved on her mind and heart. "Our whole family was there. I was almost inconsolable. We had

had too many goodbyes with dogs. It was our first foster, and we really didn't know what happened next. Would we see him again? Would he be okay? I cried because I was exhausted. I also cried because I felt so guilty to be relieved. What we had done was hard work and I felt terrible that it felt good to be relieved of it when we loved him so."

The last place that a foster family can be sure to see their warrior pup is at the final veterinary check at Holland Hospital for MWDs. Laurel, Rex, and their girls never took their eyes off EEland during the check. When the process was completed, they hugged him once more and said farewell.

EEland marched off happily to his new life in the kennels accompanied by Tracy C., the Puppy Program foster consultant who met them when they arrived.

Later, Laurel and Rex were asked if they would foster again. Laurel said they really didn't know, but then, in a few months, they picked up their next foster pup.

Like the hundreds of other patriotic families in the San Antonio area who have given so much love, time, and energy to the Foster Program, this family is now part of Lackland K9 and its global community. Rex puts it this way: "My wife and I are systems people. Lackland K9 is a life-saving system that works and we get to be a part of it." 🐾

Laurel and Rex with a foster puppy at the US Military Working Dog Teams National Monument in Lackland. FAMILY PHOTO.

UNFORGOTTEN

Months later, while EEland was still in training at Lackland, his foster family had an opportunity to see him and they wondered if he would remember them. Laurel shouldn't have worried about that. As soon as he saw them, the huge, powerful beast that had been their baby charged across the room, landed in her lap and stayed there for half an hour.

CHAPTER 3

BIG DADDY COMES HOME

Sunrise over Iraq. If you look at it just right, when nobody's trying to blow you up, it's beautiful. If you squint, you can even imagine you're back home at Lackland in south Texas—until the afternoon heat closes in.

The battle-hardened anti-terrorist they call Big Daddy knows he won't miss those extra 30 degrees of broiling heat—or the action. He supposes he's had his fill. His athleticism, bravery, and training paid off again and again. After seven tours in Iraq and Afghanistan, all this is about to end for him. He knows he will miss the camaraderie of combat.

But it's time for him to stand down. The orders give him enough time to say goodbye to the people who had supported him throughout his most recent tour. There's a lot of hugging and some tears. There's a farewell meal and then it's finally time to climb aboard the huge cargo plane and buckle in for the long journey home. The Air Force crew points the plane toward Ramstein, a NATO air base in Germany.

At Ramstein, they enjoy some schnitzel, overnight on the base, and pick up some stretcher cases from a nearby hospital. Those heroes are heading home for more treatment and to reunite with their families. Once aboard the plane, Big Daddy visits with some of the wounded. He has a knack for making others feel better. It's his nature.

Back in the States, first stop is Andrews AFB outside DELTUVAC where the stretcher cases are carefully offloaded. Some of those patients say goodbye to Big Daddy and wish him good luck in retirement.

A few hours later, his plane descends through clear blue Texas skies to touch down gently on the mammoth Lackland runway. There's a reception team at the bottom of the ramp, waiting to welcome him. Big Daddy is the embodiment of cool so he takes all of this in stride, and with gratitude. His commanding officer had ordered him to get a complete medical checkup as soon as he landed. The reception team knows the drill and drives him directly to the medical center.

The long ride back to San Antonio. PHOTO BY USAF.

On the hunt for terrorists in Iraq. PHOTO BY US ARMY STAFF SGT. MORENO, 72ND MILITARY POLICE DETACHMENT.

At the hospital, he's probed and tested. The medical director looks at him and says, "You've been through a helluva lot, but except for the battle scars you already know about, I'd say you look strong. Welcome home and welcome to your retirement. I hear a special party has been planned for you. Sorry I can't be there. Have a cold one for me."

A few days later, specially invited guests climb into pickups and SUVs for the ride to the retirement bash. In the great room, the guest of honor, Big Daddy, is the center of attention. Now formally retired, he carries himself as though he were still wearing body armor. Tall and lean, he has perfect military posture, and deep, sparkling eyes that never miss a thing. Everyone knows that his long list of missions is classified. No one asks for details. The other guests filter into the room, pay their respects to Big Daddy, and leave, hunting for refreshments.

When he was deployed, his skills were such that he was always in demand, on the run, chasing down terrorists, finding bombs, protecting his teammates, and routinely risking his own life. Now he would follow his C.O.'s advice. "Take time to slow down and smell the flowers. You've earned it."

When the last of the guests finally leaves, Big Daddy walks up to the party's hostess, and looks deeply into her eyes. She, too, has been waiting for this moment for so long. He would know her anywhere even if he were blindfolded. Her fragrance is as sweet as he had remembered. He kisses her tenderly. They sink into the cushions of the couch and she wraps herself around him. Watching all this unfold from a chair across the room, her husband, John, is smiling with satisfaction as Big Daddy begins to lick Tracy's face.

Big Daddy, also known as MWD FFalcor, is finally home to stay with the family that fostered him from puppyhood through canine adolescence. He survived battle after battle, bringing the fight to the enemy in Afghanistan and Iraq, over and over

"Big Daddy" FFalcor bites into his retirement.
PHOTO BY JANET DELTUVA.

again. His two-legged brothers-and-sisters-in-arms love and respect him. They are grateful to him for saving their lives on many occasions and he knows it. It is, after all, what he was born to do. It is now his time to relax, to snuggle with those who have always adored him and to have his very own place on that wonderful, comfy couch between Tracy and John.

FFalcor's post-retirement life has blessed Lackland with dozens of fine sons and daughters. His bloodline of US Defense Department Puppy Program dogs is on guard around the world, securing our military bases and walking in front of our anti-terrorist units to make their extremely dangerous job safer in a time of increasing threat. At Lackland, FFalcor can be found napping in Tracy's office. But don't be fooled by his closed eyes. His nose and ears are on duty. He's quite alert, just in case. After all, you can take the dog out of the fight, but not the fight out of the dog. 🐾

CHAPTER 4

UNPREDICTABLE

"I love HHarpy and did from the moment they put her in my arms," says Nancy R., an experienced and committed member of the Lackland foster community. "There is literally nothing I would not do for this dog. Even before she completed her almost half year foster time with us, my husband and I were utterly convinced that HHarpy would be the best MWD candidate the Breeding Program had ever seen," Nancy recalls. "We just knew that one day, she would leap out of helicopters with her handler, that she would lead her troops safely around IEDs, and bravely defend them against ambushes." But it was not to be. "Our HHarpy showed all the signs of success—until she actually reported for duty at Lackland."

Uncontrollable HHarpy washed out of Puppy School and returned home to Nancy and her husband. "She is an excellent example of a dog that washed out, not because she lacked the drives to hunt and fight, but because she lacked the required focus to use her drives only when ordered," explains Nancy as she strokes HHarpy's neck. "And she is not an easy dog to live with even after over a year of private training with a highly regarded instructor. She is much better than she had been but she will always be unreliable and she must wear a muzzle in public."

NATURE AND NURTURE

What is challenging for canine geneticists is that submissive dogs and aggressive dogs can be offspring of the same hero war dogs and be raised in the same loving way by the same family. What remains constant and reliable though is the endless dedication of the fosters who are always alert to the possibility of the unpredictable.

When HHarpy entered their lives, veteran fosters Gary and Nancy saw every sign of an emerging champion. FAMILY PHOTO.

RRudy coming out of the pool. FAMILY PHOTO.

HHarpy loves to play in the pool and is also very possessive of it, despite her fosters' best efforts to get her to share. "We don't have anyone else, human or canine, enter the water when she is swimming. We tried but couldn't train the aggressive possessiveness out of her. It started when she was still a tiny foster, but it got much stronger as an adult. She also has several medical issues that have cost us a great deal of money. But she is our HHarpy and we love her."

Unlike HHarpy, Gary and Nancy's first foster had no problem learning to focus and control her power. "Her name is CCorryn. She hooked us on fostering these special dogs within a day of being in our home. She was wonderful and had none of Harpy's control issues. She learned obedience quickly and socialized easily. She was gentle and kind with strangers. No muzzle required," Nancy says.

Despite her many good qualities, CCoryn ultimately did not meet all the requirements to become an MWD. "As with a considerable number of Lackland washouts," Gary explains, "CCoryn became a civilian police department K9 officer."

Nancy and Gary's third foster is a very stable Mal called KKhloe. Nancy says this warrior pup is a delight. "She is totally calm even with little kids she meets on walks. But she is very serious about balls and won't leave the pool until she has successfully retrieved the one thrown for her." DTS trainers told Gary and Nancy that KKhloe is the superstar of her litter. Today, she is a dual-purpose, fully certified MWD on guard with our troops. Gary and Nancy gave her a great start, including introducing her to the outside world with its unpredictable sights and sounds. "That's one of the agreed upon tasks every foster promises to do," smiles Gary, "Any visit to the supermarket can end up being quite an event because these pups attract a lot of attention.

While warrior pups are growing up in foster care, they often lead lives of luxury, as can be seen in this photo of Nancy's fourth foster, RRudy, discovered at the pool as though awaiting his monogrammed robe before heading for his cabana.

Gary and Nancy's fifth foster is UUrzua. Today he is admired as an MWD, but it wasn't an easy journey getting him there. Gary and Nancy had early indicators of possible trouble ahead. By the time UUrzua was barely six months old, Gary had to use a muzzle every time he gave the increasingly assertive dog a bath.

UUrzua enjoying bite work with his handler at Camp Pendleton. US MARINE CORPS PHOTO BY LANCE CPL. BRADLEY J. MORROW.

At the end of the almost six months as a foster pup, UUrzua entered Puppy School and did well. But in Dog Training School he repeatedly bit his instructors and was kicked out. It took Doc weeks of persistent intensive training to transform the powerful but unstable critter into the completely reliable war dog he was to become. He was readmitted to DTS and no longer bit his instructors.

UUrzua eventually passed the rigorous certification tests for explosives detection and patrol including attack-on-command. When he shipped out to his first duty station, he was met by his first handler—a young Marine. As his justifiably proud foster mom declared, "Our UUrzua is now a United States Marine and destined for some very serious work protecting our troops!"

UUrzua adores his handler and places his big paw on his handler's boot as though saying, "This is mine."
PHOTO BY SERGEANT 1ST CLASS SUZANNE RINGLE, USMC.

Their sixth foster is one of those rare Belgian Malinois warrior pups born with no apparent courage, even though his lineage is fierce and that trait is usually passed on to the next generation. When Nancy and Gary took little ZZorn to the national monument to Military Working Dog Teams, he seemed intimidated.

"His reaction to the big bronze dog at the monument was one of great concern," Gary explains. "He immediately gets submissive when startled or in the presence of something new." This behavior pattern eliminated ZZorn from serving in the military or in law enforcement. He's enjoying a quiet suburban life as a very gentle house pet. 🐾

CHAPTER 5

THE CROONER

Love is the critical ingredient in the Lackland K9 magic that creates America's highly effective Military Working Dogs. Every year, roughly 270 newly trained dogs are required from Lackland by the Defense Department for assignments around the world in the navy, army, air force, and marines.

In a narrow hallway of a small building at Lackland Air Force Base, a tall man in camo and sandals sits cross-legged on the floor. He repeatedly tosses a set of keys a few yards in front of him, encouraging a very young puppy to give chase. After a while, the puppy leaps forward with increasing enthusiasm. Two things are immediately apparent: The puppy loves the game, and the man loves the dog. What isn't obvious is that this man is engaged in a focused effort designed to bring out the baby dog's natural drive to chase and hold. Those are crucial drives if a puppy is going to become a MWD. To bring out those drives, the man is wielding enormous knowledge, experience, and love.

A lot of that magic emanates from the guy playing with the puppy. That's Stewart H., PhD. Everyone at Lackland calls him "Doc." He's the US Air Force's top dog trainer and a renowned expert in canine behavioral psychology. He is also the manager of the Defense Department's Military Working Dog Breeding Program. For Doc, connecting with a dog's innate love for humans is at the very core of the mystical bond between warrior pups and their handlers. That love, plus meticulous care and consistency in training is the full formula for the Lackland Magic.

Spend enough time with him, and you'll learn a tremendous amount from Doc. After a while, you disappear into the background because his focus on his dogs is so intense and there are so many dogs for whom he is responsible. Whether he is flying with his team to meet with dog brokers in Amsterdam to select another group of candidates for the Dog Training School or gently comforting a beautiful baby Mal from his Military Working Dog Breeding Program, Doc is pursuing the central passion of his life. He began training protection dogs using the traditional European system called Schutzhund when he was still a teenager.

Early bite work instruction led by "Doc" Stewart H. PHOTO BY JANET DELTUVA.

TRAINING SHOULD BE FUN

Training is a constant throughout a Military Working Dog's life, from Puppy School through advanced, highly realistic, pre-deployment training, which helps a dog and handler team prepare for being inserted into combat operations. Wherever it occurs, Doc teaches that training needs to be varied, challenging, and fun. Dogs, like their human handlers, can become bored by routine. To get maximum performance from our K9s, trainers need to keep it interesting.

Sometimes a future war dog just needs a reassuring hug.
PHOTO BY LESLIE STONE-KAMEN.

If Doc has his way, that sweet puppy in his arms will enjoy her almost half year in foster care followed by her formal training experience and grow into a bodacious beast of a Military Working Dog. If you had walked past Doc as he held that pup, you would have heard him quietly crooning, "Good puppers, good puppers, good puppers." It's a lot like the sound a father makes to reassure his human baby that she is adored and safe.

Doc would strongly object to being called a dog whisperer. So, let's just say he's a very gifted trainer who cares enormously about each dog under his care. After all, it is Doc who selectively breeds each generation of homegrown warrior pups for maximum strength, agility, intelligence, and courage so they can graduate the canine basic training course before they are two years old.

After rigorous testing, Doc and his crew certify that the dogs have learned the basic skills of patrol and odor detection. Then the 341st Training Squadron ships the dogs out to their home

Doc helps build a pup's natural ball drive, which is a precursor to patrol training. PHOTO BY JANET DELTUVA.

bases across the nation and around the world. There they meet their first handlers and receive the beginning of their advanced training as well as daily refreshers on the basics. The photo on page 26 shows little QQuantico learning to seek inside a drawer; he's hunting for a piece of kibble.

Doc's formula for successful training is a meticulously nuanced mix of loving kindness, brief intense instruction, praise, repetition, more praise, and lots of brief rewards that help build the warrior pups' drives to seek and fight. All these skills are learned under tight trainer control.

It takes about a year of very careful training for Doc and his team to turn a seven-month-old Belgian Malinois puppy from the Breeding Program into a Military Working Dog with basic skills. That year includes two components, the foundational Puppy School followed by the more advanced 120-day Dog Training School, where they train alongside the imported dogs who arrive from Europe four times a year to help fill the Pentagon's global requirement for MWDs.

Warrior pup QQuantico learns to search and winds up inside a drawer. Today, he's a Marine. FAMILY PHOTO.

Doc says he breeds for specific traits. "We are looking for a puppy who's very steady and bold and will experience our training as fun!" Whether they are born at Lackland or overseas, Doc's ultimate goal is the creation of a remarkable K9. "He's got to be a dog we can wake up in the middle of the night. A dog that can be calm when he's taken by a bunch of people wearing 'battle rattle,' which is all the equipment a combat soldier has to wear. He's also a dog who isn't frightened by the noise of a helicopter," says Doc.

Aboard that helicopter, the soldiers are in what Doc calls action mode. "They're headed to a place where they might get killed or their teammates might get killed. This tense mood communicates itself to everyone involved, especially the dog." When the helicopter lands, and the team jumps out, the dog has to be able to function immediately. As Doc explains, "The handler says to his canine partner, 'Here we go! Time to work!' Then that dog has to be happy, cheerful, and what we call 'drivey.' He has to want to find hidden IEDs, guns, ammo, and bad guys, and he has to warn his troops of ambushes. That dog has to be the kind of extraordinary animal for whom this whole stressful scene is exciting and fun, and the only thing he wants to do is his job."

What is natural to these herding dogs is that they want to run, hunt, fight, and depend deeply on one human being. That's where the training begins to refine, amplify, and control the dog's natural impulses. Doc insists that "Before you can expect a dog to be interested in training or working, the dog must be healthy and happy and feel an emotional bond with its trainer."

Along with having its fundamental needs for shelter, food, and safety met, warrior pups must play or they will not train well. In Doc's words, "Carefree and happy play between dog and handler is a vital part of a healthy and productive training relationship."

All the training of new dogs at Lackland starts with the building of rapport between trainers and dogs. Treated properly—and at Lackland they are—the dogs joyfully respond to every opportunity to work, which they regard as play. At the same time, they are highly sensitive to emotions and read humans immediately. As a result, Doc says it is mandatory for trainers to be "positive and enthusiastic around the dogs they are training because that is exactly what we need back from the dogs—positive response to training and enthusiasm for everything we ask them to do."

Doc insists that volunteers who foster expose the little furry future heroes to a wide variety of different environments and places including restaurants, ballgames, parades, crowds of people, noisy places, elevators, stairs, and slick linoleum or tile floors. "Environmental conditioning is crucial for your puppy's development," Doc says. "The idea is to gradually expose the pup to more intense stimuli and situations, all the while keeping it comfortable and curious rather than frightening the little dog."

There are some real "don'ts" which fosters must observe. One of them is instructive for all of us who have very young dogs: "Puppies should not participate in sustained running because that kind of repeated pounding is too harsh for their soft, developing bones and joints." Then there is that taboo that speaks to the difference between raising a pet and raising a warrior pup: water bottles. "Puppies love to play with plastic water bottles. However, potable water for our military personnel comes in plastic bottles, and discarded empty bottles are a common feature of deployed areas. If a full-grown MWD sees a bottle as a toy he can become distracted from his work, " and that can be the difference between life and death for the squad he's protecting.

Watching Doc and his team of gifted trainers work with warrior pups is inspiring and reveals his philosophy in action. Of course, the team has its standard operating procedures, but when needed there is specialized training available, carefully tailored to the unique needs of an otherwise promising pup. 🐾

MWD all grown up! QQuantico and handler Sgt. Josh J. guarding Marine One, the helicopter of the president of the United States. PHOTO COURTESY USMC SGT. JOSH J.

CHAPTER 6

BERNIE'S KIDS

Who wouldn't want her job? Bernie G. is getting paid to play with puppies! At least that's how it may appear at first. But when you watch Bernie in action for more than a few minutes, you start to notice that what looks like play is really a series of carefully observed interactions. This is demanding work that requires knowledge, experience, and talent. It's designed to reveal the early signs of a puppy's character and personality as well as its comfort level with humans.

Each puppy born in the breeding program has a name and a number, and the highly trained staff keeps track of its development. About fifteen litters of new puppies are born at Lackland's Military Working Dog Breeding Program every year. The staff engages with the puppies to gauge their emerging personalities as part of Doc's carefully designed system. Each of these critters costs the taxpayer about thirty thousand dollars from birth through advanced training and each of them is a life-saving defensive military system-in-the-making.

For someone who adores dogs and is totally committed to doing everything possible to protect US troops, Bernie has the best job ever. She's a highly respected member of the US military K9 community. Bernie is a gifted trainer

> ## NOT HOUSE DOGS
>
> The dogs the Defense Department breeds or buys come from bloodlines of bold, aggressive hunters. "That's the kind of dog we can train to protect our troops," says Bernie. "These dogs are born to fight, and we encourage that, but we control their aggression through training. Military Working Dogs are taught to do on command the thing which we tell our pet dogs never to do—show aggression to people."

Bernie G. with some of the puppies who were bred to be US MWDs.
PHOTO BY JANET DELTUVA.

A trainer gives her Mal a pep talk before a repeat test of response to gunfire. PHOTO BY JEFF KAMEN.

Bernie says, "The fundamentals of daily obedience training—including 'sit,' 'stay,' and 'heel'—are the pathways to specialized instruction in aggression control."

Two weeks later, Bernie is conducting Dog Training School certification examinations in a grassy area between two long buildings used for interior search training exercises. Instructors are taking turns walking their canine students up to Bernie. She writes down the name of the dog and its trainer before she tests the dog on a spectrum of skills, including obedience and reaction to gunfire. Almost twenty-four weeks have passed since they entered the Dog Training School and by now, all of the warrior pups in this class of 270 dogs have been carefully trained to ignore some of the elements of the chaos of battle. A dog cannot be certified if it does not remain neutral in the presence of these sounds. Otherwise, at first contact with the enemy, the dog can be distracted and fail to work.

During the certification evaluations, a talented young instructor is seen on the sidelines in what appears to be a confidence-building conversation with one of the dogs she's training. A few minutes later, that trainer is in front of Bernie with the same dog and a pistol that fires blank rounds. The trainer fires round after round. The dog has no observable reactions. The instructor beams as Bernie flashes her famous, dimpled smile and exclaims, "Well done!" Only the week before the same dog had startled when the gun went off. Of course, things don't always go so well. Another young trainer is clearly heartbroken

Bernie is elated that this dog has passed its obedience certification test. PHOTO BY JEFF KAMEN.

after one of his dogs fails to pass a critical test. Bernie gives the trainer a second chance, but it's clear the pup simply isn't ready. Bernie tells the trainer what he must do to help the dog make the grade, and one week later, it's smooth sailing for the dog and trainer.

Bernie's sign-off on this warrior pup's crucial certification is part of the process that sends him from Lackland to his permanent home base and the beginning of his life of adventure and service. The warrior pups who make it really love the work they were born, raised and trained to do. Just like Bernie. 🐾

OUT!

A properly trained Military Working Dog might be calmly receiving a good scratch from its handler as you walk by. But if the handler orders you to stop and shouts, "Watch him!" the dog will suddenly turns its focus onto you, waiting for the command to bite. When the handler shouts, "Out!" the MWD will immediately stand down. That is controlled aggression.

CHAPTER 7

THE MUSICIANS

No matter where our troops are, US military bands entertain them, and that can mean flying into potentially dangerous areas to boost morale. Drum major USAF Master Sergeant Darrin D. and his clarinetist wife, Air Force Staff Sergeant Lenora D., know all about this lifestyle. Sometimes it means finding yourself in a hazardous situation overseas; other times it's enjoying really good tacos in San Antonio. Having similar backgrounds helps. Like Darrin, Lenora comes from a family of American military heroes. She's a high-energy Midwesterner with a penchant for getting things done.

The only thing this couple loves more than music and each other is the Military Working Dog Breeding Program at Lackland, where they and the rest of the Air Force Band of the West are based. They could never have imagined that their early interest in fostering a puppy would lead them to become important players in the ongoing success of the MWD Breeding Program.

On a brilliantly sunlit day, Lenora and Darrin are in civilian clothes, volunteering at an exciting air show at Randolph Air Force Base in San Antonio. They are on the lookout for dog-loving

HAPPY WARRIORS

Darrin and Lenora D. have fostered nine warrior pups. Several of their babies are on duty around the world guarding military bases and protecting troops. ZZumwalt and HHilda, two Lackland washouts, have become their devoted house pets. ZZumwalt is a charmer. Just don't leave him alone with your computer unless you really want to test how protective the case is.

Darrin and Lenora were recognized for their volunteer support of the 341st Training Squadron, USAF, which runs the Breeding Program. PHOTO BY JANET DELTUVA.

Lenora and Darrin carry MMurphy, a handsome warrior pup, as bait to draw in potential fosters. PHOTO BY JEFF KAMEN.

families who might be interested in joining the ranks of the Puppy Breeding Program's volunteer foster program. More than fifty thousand people have arrived at the sprawling airbase to visit some of the world's largest military aircraft, get a closer look at a Predator drone, and line up for Texas-style refreshments. The musicians carry MMurphy, a handsome warrior pup, as bait to draw in potential fosters. Meanwhile, the sky overhead fills with silver and blue fighter planes from a bygone era, engaged in a meticulously choreographed dogfight. It's all great fun.

Hundreds of visitors make their way from the runway to a nearby area where Military Working Dogs are performing bite demonstrations with their very well-trained human decoys (their trainers). Of course, the decoys are wearing thickly padded bite suits. Still, when a decoy is knocked down and bitten by a dog, the crowd responds with awe.

Like all fosters, Darrin and Lenora's home had to be approved by a Department of Defense Breeding Program staffer, who checks for required air conditioning, door locks, screened windows, and secure

New foster families are needed every year. They get to take home adorable critters like these two.
U.S. AIR FORCE PHOTO/TECHNICAL SERGEANT BENNIE J. DAVIS III.

property fences. Afterall, warrior pups are national security assets. Military Working Dogs are the only weapon system that depends on a major *volunteer* component for its creation. Some foster families are civilians while others are currently serving in the military or are retired from the service. They come from all ranks. At foster events, however, they call one another by first names and exchange experiences and advice to support each other's success in raising future K9 heroes. The foster community ethos strongly reflects the noble Air Force motto, "Service Before Self."

Fosters receive their puppies at a formal briefing where they get detailed marching orders and an even more detailed guidebook to follow. Before Lenora and Darrin created the closed Facebook page that now allows fosters to help one another 24/7, there was no organized place for them to communicate with each other. Their Facebook page is all about information sharing, puppy training events, and supporting their community. It's become essential to the well-being of the puppies as well as to the sanity of sometimes desperately overwhelmed fosters. "Our Facebook page," Lenora says, "has turned into a place people visit to commiserate when things are tough and to get help when they're frustrated. Or when they need a puppy sitter even on an emergency basis. You can't leave your Breeding Program Puppy with anyone but another cleared foster. That's a firm rule." The Facebook page and the community it creates also allow people to support one another even in matters that don't have anything to do with dogs. When the elderly mother of one of the fosters became ill, for example, other fosters rose to help by providing food, transportation, respite care, and a loving sense of being connected.

Many fosters become friends and spend social time together. Lively conversation at those parties revolves around the dogs. Lenora and Darrin created "Cry Baby Dinners" to comfort those fosters who are facing turn-in time. That's when their little warrior pup is returned to Lackland for the beginning of formal training and life in the kennels.

Darrin and Lenora's Facebook page provides crucial support to the Lackland Breeding Program's two foster consultants, a pair of veteran dog handlers who have seen it all. These two professionals respond to the most urgent calls from new fosters, schedule home visits, and manage veterinary appointments. Their schedules are full and would be a lot less manageable without Lenora and Darrin's Facebook community and personal involvement.

By their very nature these super-charged highly athletic puppies are sometimes hazardous to themselves and others in unpredictable ways. With the help of the Facebook page, highly experienced fosters like Lenora and Darrin and a dozen others who have been through every imaginable challenge carry on a continuing dialogue with new fosters, helping them navigate the unexpected intricacies of their sometimes staggering new responsibilities.

Darrin and Lenora advise new fosters on a broad range of practical issues. When serious medical matters arise, they refer them to the foster consultants and to Holland Hospital for MWDs at Lackland where Army veterinarians are always available. That is why all fosters must live within two hours' drive of the base.

Lenora and Darrin work hard at being effective Air Force diplomats for the Puppy Program. They forge relationships of trust with trainers and handlers. They pay close attention to new fosters, following up on their requests for help—sometimes in just minutes. Even when they have had an exhausting day at work, they convey kindness and patience when they deal with other fosters. However, if they come to believe that a pup's welfare is in jeopardy because a new foster isn't measuring up, they don't hesitate to alert the Breeding Program staff, which is empowered to re-home the pup. "Thankfully, it doesn't happen often," Darrin says, "and that

Foster parent Annie A. gets her latest pup, and it's bliss every time! PHOTO BY JANET DELTUVA.

shows how attentive and caring the vast majority of fosters truly are." Thanks to Lenora and Darrin D., fosters get to benefit from a connected, caring community rather than struggling in isolation. 🐾

CHAPTER 8

HELP IS HERE!

If you're a puppy or a horse or a human being who needs help, she will drive through a storm in the middle of the Texas night to be at your side. That's her nature, and Puppy Breeding Program staffer Tracy C. makes it all look easy. It is her steadfast loving response that draws animals and people to her and makes them feel safe. Her ability to bring calm amidst chaos is essential. She spends her day in the often erratic company of fierce dogs, quirky puppies, and stressed out people. The hundred new babies born every year at Lackland's Puppy Breeding Program and their volunteer foster families have first dibs on Tracy's time.

She is one of two Breeding Program foster consultants who serve as educators and trouble-shooters for the program. When it's time to prepare new foster families for the realities of their almost six months of challenging responsibility, Tracy—a trained veterinary technician—is often in charge of getting them to pay close attention to the detailed directions that all fosters must promise to follow. Later, if a puppy has an urgent problem that is more than a new foster family can handle, Tracy stops whatever is going on in her life and heads to the trouble. In many ways, she embodies the fierce love that is the hallmark of the Military Working Dog world.

Tracy and her husband John live less than an hour's drive from Lackland on a small ranch. Here, rattlesnakes, scorpions, and three varieties of poisonous spiders slither in the shade of elegant twenty-foot-tall century agave plants.

Long before roosters announce the beginning of a new day, Tracy is wide awake in the dark, feeding, watering, and exercising three horses, eleven adopted dogs, and three cats. For Tracy, life is all about the joy of doing what must be done for her family menagerie, for the Department of Defense's Military Working Dog Breeding Program, and maybe, most of all, for FFalcor. He is the foster puppy who came home after many years at war to curl up with his foster mom for the rest of his life.

Retired MWD FFalcor with his mom, Puppy Breeding Program staffer Tracy C.
PHOTO BY JANET DELTUVA.

FFalcor seems very much at home during a visit to the US Military Working Dog Teams National Monument at Lackland. PHOTO BY LESLIE STONE-KAMEN.

These days, one of FFalcor's breed-signature ears is a bit crumpled, the result of a mix of hard, adventurous work in dangerous places and the process of aging. When this large, dominant Belgian Malinois was sent into harm's way to protect our troops, both of his ears had stood at attention, alert to sounds human ears are unable to hear. This includes the subtle noises terrorists make when they are waiting to ambush our troops. FFalcor heard those tiny noises, and smelled the odors of their bodies. Detecting those odors caused him to alert by immediately lying down with his nose pointed toward the center of the scent cone, the invisible and

PASSING OF THE TORCH

In 2015, FFalcor retired from being the Breeding Program's leading man. He went back home for good with his mama.

most intense point of odor emanation. Whenever he detected one of those human odors or the smell of hidden explosives and pointed to it, FFalcor's beloved handler, the very center of his life, would make that happy sound—"Good boy!"—delivered in an uplifted voice, and give him his favorite toy to chew on for a while.

Between setting up medical visits, managing turn-ins, and fielding orders from Doc, Tracy reminisces about the young FFalcor. "He was a quiet puppy, very quiet and very intense. He is still quiet and intense and he still has the same look on his face which can seem menacing. I think that is what made a lot of people nervous as he got bigger. What I tried to explain to some of the other handlers so that they could get along with him is that he is kind of like *Star Trek*'s Mr. Spock. He's got the same face when he is happy and when he is sad. He is just a super powerful dog but that does not mean that he wants to hurt anybody."

FFalcor first entered Tracy's life eight years earlier. "I got him at eight weeks old," Tracy recalls as she slides her fingers along the thick fur and muscle of FFalcor's neck. The big guy looks up adoringly at her from his place on the couch. "A soldier who was also a trainer at the Dog Training School was fostering FFalcor," Tracy remembers. "He would bring this unusually intense puppy to work and leave him with me at the Breeding Program office during the day. Whenever I had a break, I spent time with him."

Then, one day, the trainer hurt his back, which is a common injury among Dog Training School instructors. "They are out there training all day long," Tracy said, "and these are crazy strong, still undisciplined dogs. You think you've got one of these pups under control. Then he suddenly surges and you're tossed against a wall or a truck or into a doorjamb. Part of the job. But for this poor guy, the pain was so bad, it was impossible for him to raise the puppy."

Tracy ended up taking FFalcor home to her ranch. "In my life, that is not an uncommon practice. Somebody gets hurt; I get a puppy for a while. This time, I ended up with FFalcor for most of his puppy life."

Back from his deployments, FFalcor began enjoying his retirement, which included the kind of post-combat mission many soldiers dream about. Tracy noted with a smile of motherly pride that her boy was "a favorite of the ladies in the Breeding Program." He is the papa of ninety Defense Department puppies.

Today, FFalcor lives with some residual pain but still radiates power. Even after a series of surgeries for combat-related wounds, the old retired Military Working Dog inspires respect and

Tracy and FFalcor. PHOTO BY JEFF KAMEN.

fear in other dogs. People who are not totally self-involved sense something strong as he passes them on the street.

For now, she can relax. They are in the back room of a pizza joint in suburban San Antonio with a group of other fosters and their pups. FFalcor is eyeing the sausage and meatball with extra cheese. Tracy offers him a small bite, which he accepts with remarkable care and gentleness.

Tracy has invited a photographer to the informal gathering. He has heard about the great war dog but this is his first encounter. As FFalcor approaches, the cameraman remembers not to stare into the canine's eyes, not to smile showing teeth, or to make a sudden move (like suddenly swinging a camera into position). Among dogs, all three of those actions can be triggers to a fight. Tracy whispers something to FFalcor, who sizes up the photographer, and then leans into the sitting man's leg—a sign of acceptance. The photographer greets FFalcor with a calm voice and pets the big dog.

STILL A WARRIOR

Tracy has a high level of situational awareness. She never takes her eyes off their surroundings when they are in public. She is never casual about her grip on his thick, military leash. She knows that if FFalcor were to detect what he perceives as a threat to her, he would overcome his pain and remember his training.

Later that night, FFalcor is bedded down inside his crate house next to Tracy's side of a king-size bed. As the photographer is leaving the family ranch, a younger very high energy Malinois comes flying at him, growling menacingly, bouncing to a halt against a cyclone fence. The unflappable Tracy laughs and explains that the angry dog is "a perfectly sweet boy except for those moments when he sees a stranger, or he just goes completely cuckoo. He's one of the few loons the Puppy Breeding Program has produced. There's nothing to worry about. I've got it covered."

She always does. 🐾

CHAPTER 9

VICTORIOUS WASHOUT

From the moment she was first able to move beyond the loving warmth of her mommy and the rest of her litter, the puppy named NNoel was a standout. She was an especially sweet girl, full of fun and very inquisitive. When she got used to her legs, she bounded toward every human that came near her, tail wagging, eyes twinkling. All signs pointed to emerging boldness and self-confidence. It was clear to the pros at Lackland that this tiny warrior pup was on her way to big things.

She was a happy foster and a star in puppy school. Dog Training School was right around the corner. Then, in one of the strangest quirks in the veterinary history of Lackland, NNoel was bitten on a foreleg by a Texas-sized spider. The puppy had what may have been an allergic reaction. That bite left her sick for a long time in Holland Hospital for Military Working Dogs only yards from the kennels. Despite the best efforts of the Holland team, the determination was made that the spider had not only interrupted but ruined NNoel's career as a potential Military Working Dog. NNoel was not happy being in the hospital or the kennels. She wanted to do things. She needed to work!

LOVER AND FIGHTER

Her name changed but not her personality. She is a total sweetheart—when she isn't working. On the job, however, Corporal Neeva is one tough street cop says Clint! Neeva's partner/dad is justifiably proud of his baby girl: "She is very fast, has extreme prey drive, is one of the most effective narcotics detection dogs I have ever met. Many other handlers who have seen her in action, agree."

NNoel washed out of Lackland to become a law enforcement superstar.
PHOTO COURTESY CLINT WOOD.

CHAPTER 10

THE PSYCHOTHERAPIST

Elizabeth M. is in the fight to save our troops any way she can. She is a former Army medic who became a psychotherapist and now works at the Veterans Administration Hospital in San Antonio, where she devotes herself to helping our combat veterans heal from post-traumatic stress disorder (PTSD). Elizabeth's experience with PTSD patients compelled her to begin fostering future MWDs.

"These dogs," says Elizabeth, "are all about prevention. Every dog that discovers an IED, or sniffs out an ambush, also prevents people from developing PTSD. Those soldiers the dogs save from IEDS don't have to come to me later wrapped in agony. The pain I see in my patients is so deep, so complicated, even the most courageous of them can feel hopelessly trapped in it."

Elizabeth was inspired to get involved with Lackland K9s when she saw a news story on television about the power of MWDs to detect IEDs. At first she thought she could never be a foster, to share so much love with a puppy and let him go at the end of six months, but then she saw another news story in which the Puppy Breeding Program was appealing for more help from the local community.

"That did it," she says. "I shoved aside my selfishness. I found the strength I would need to return the puppy to the program when it was time."

Elizabeth put in an application and waited for several weeks until she got a phone call to schedule a home visit. People from the program came to check her out as well as her kids and her house. "We must have passed their tests," she says, "because the next week, I got a phone call that they had a puppy who needed to change foster homes. I was so excited to pick up my first puppy. Her name is NNikki."

Even though NNikki was a cute puppy with a floppy ear, things didn't go precisely the way Elizabeth had envisioned. "Talk about appearances being deceiving! She was simply horrible.

When Breeding Program staffer Josh D. hands you a puppy, it can take a few days before you find out if the dog is an angel or a demon. Elizabeth M. has welcomed them all into her home. PHOTO BY JANET DELTUVA.

Elizabeth and her latest foster, NNariko. PHOTO BY JEFF KAMEN.

She was over-reactive, really impulsive, and rude. She bit every member of my family. During Thanksgiving, she bit my mother, ripped up her watch, and ate a quilt! She was a bad dog. But I loved her. Now she's living with a retired US Army handler in Oklahoma on a lot of land surrounded by tall fences that keep her in!"

The next puppy, SSophia, was the complete opposite of NNikki. Elizabeth describes her as "very loving and very intense. She listened and was super athletic and eager to please! But she had no sense of self-protection at all. She jumped off a retaining wall. She climbed a large oak tree and

NNikki the "bad" dog. FAMILY PHOTO.

fell off. She did some crazy Malligator stuff, too, like ripping out some of our plumbing." SSophia is now a Marine serving at an air station in Japan. "I understand she's doing very well," Elizabeth says proudly. "She's a patrol and detection dog and also in a helicopter unit."

TTabitha was Elizabeth's third foster puppy. A smart, stable dog, she's now a training aide, helping to teach new handler candidates how to do their jobs. The next Breeding Program pup to join Elizabeth's household was ZZigane. That's Hungarian for gypsy. "She's my gypsy girl now," says Elizabeth, "because ZZigane flunked out of DTS and I gave her a forever home with us. She got kicked out because she has no focusable attack drive. She's not wired to learn to attack on command. She only likes to bite when she wants to."

Some of Elizabeth's fosters. There's TTabitha (top left), who's a training aide, SSophia (top right) who's now a patrol dog, and NNariko (bottom right), Elizabeth's current foster. FAMILY PHOTOS.

Like every Belgian Malinois, ZZigane requires a lot of exercise. Elizabeth learned that she can take her to a park, but she's got to be on high alert when she does. "ZZigane likes bikes, kids, runners, and strollers. And when I say like, I mean she wants to take them down and bite them! Of course, she's on a leash and I don't let her get near anyone. Still, it is so embarrassing to me. It's as if she'll select the weakest-looking person in the park and then clearly want to go after them!"

Elizabeth's current foster is NNariko. She was such a big puppy, she was the only one in the litter. "She just turned twelve weeks," says Elizabeth. "She's an awesome dog. She has a lot of ball and prey drive. She loves to bite. She's afraid of nothing. Nothing. Sometimes, she deliberately knocks things over and then looks at me defiantly as if to say, 'What have you got for me now, huh?'" Elizabeth hopes NNariko will grow up to save many soldiers from the kinds of horror that create PTSD. 🐾

CHAPTER 11

LEARNING A NEW WAY

Mike B. and his family have come to love the Breeding Program and are delighted that they can be truly helpful by fostering and by enlisting new families into this effort. Mike's home, an hour outside of San Antonio, is often a gathering place for other fosters and their dogs. To show you how much he loves these dogs, Mike even has a dog bone–shaped pool, which is open to people and their critters.

Mike initially joined the foster program thinking that he and his family would enjoy a never-ending stream of fabulous free puppies while doing a good thing for the nation. As Mike says, "Puppies are really cool. Who doesn't like puppies for God's sake?"

Mike had already proven to himself that he had a special rapport with dogs. "My Rhodesian Ridgeback, Dixie, spent numerous years accompanying me to nursing homes. I'm a physical therapist and have worked at several dozen homes. Dixie worked off-leash almost exclusively. She stayed when I told her to, put her head in someone's lap for petting when I told her to, and ignored food on the floor. Like I said, I'm 'good' with dogs."

> ### TAKE THAT!
>
> **Fierce possessiveness is a mandatory trait for an MWD. It's necessary for the dog to stay on the odor of an explosive he detects until he's released by his handler. The same thing applies to a suspect he captures. If a warrior pup does not immediately show strong possessiveness as part of his personality, Doc and his team use special playing techniques to build the intensity of that crucial canine drive.**

Mike B. with a Breeding Program puppy he and his family raised as part of the foster program. PHOTO BY JANET DELTUVA.

Mike knows that one day a puppy he's fostered may have to be carried out of combat wrapped around his handler's neck. So he starts getting them used to this early. PHOTO BY JEFF KAMEN.

Mike introducing a Breeding Program puppy to people attending an air show in San Antonio. PHOTO BY JEFF KAMEN.

Mike vividly remembers his family's first puppy orientation at Lackland and his own attitude at that event. "They instructed us on the intensity of the breed. Right, I thought, it's just a dog. They taught us incentive training. I was completely blown away," said Mike. "Treat training, I thought, was the realm of the big box pet stores and of the whacko animal rights folks who support a Zen-like relationship with your dog."

That wasn't Mike's way. He was old school, deeply steeped in coercion training. "It had worked wonderfully for me. My dogs were confident and unafraid. They did what I asked, always. But, this time it was the Defense Department's puppy. I'm a team player and I

PHOTO BY JEFF KAMEN.

decided I'll do what they require. So, we take home this lovely Breeding Program puppy, AAllen, and he's full of energy."

As some professional trainers say, "Human pride goeth before a Malinois." Mike tells how a very small Mal taught him an unexpected lesson in humility: "My first clue that I truly had no clue was when I attempted the typical wrestle-with-your-dog play. You gently shake the dog's head, spin him around and roll him over on his back." This is a dominance game and it establishes who's boss through play. Mike expected "a friendly jump into my arms and a resulting cuddle. Instead, I was the recipient of a full-on lunge with a snapping alligator-mouth bite. This seven-week-old pup was saying, 'Game on! This is what I do!' With his baby teeth and his fierce Malinois attitude, he drew my blood." Not a lot, but enough to really get Mike's attention.

WALL OF SHAME

At puppy orientation, new fosters are told about a vet tech's Wall of Shame, and how you really don't want to be on it. The wall contains an array of objects that had to be surgically removed from puppies' digestive tracts, including rocks and metal screws. Curious young Mals love to learn about their world by first biting and then swallowing whatever they discover.

What followed is what Mike calls life-changing comprehension. "Turns out I wasn't good with dogs, I was good with *easy* dogs. This foster pup from the Breeding Program was another thing, entirely! I would need a new approach. Theirs."

So he began following the Fostering Manual training standard, which is all based on loving, positive reinforcement. Mike also took note of the Breeding Program's warning to be on your guard against any imaginable trouble, including the fast-moving puppy suddenly swallowing almost anything.

One evening, Mike was working on a patient report for work when he heard the reassuring sound of the pup chewing on a supposedly indestructible chew toy. All was well. Then, after a while, Mike noticed that things had gotten quiet. Too quiet. "I got up to investigate. The pup had just chewed a hole in the carpet in the other room. That was a twenty-five hundred dollar situational awareness failure on my part!"

Fostering can drain all your energy. You have to be vigilant about what the pup is doing any time he's not locked safely in his crate house. According to Mike, "Your inner clock triggers a small panic if the dog is out of sight for thirty seconds, even for fifteen seconds."

At one of the regular training sessions for fosters, Doc lectured on how to get a pup to drop an object. You offer them something else fast. Mike's foster, HHengst, decided to help him understand that lesson in a visceral way that Mike says he will never forget. "The pup picked up a rather large frog. I panicked and shouted 'No!' and chased him into the garage. He looked up at me from underneath my compressor and swallowed the frog whole. HHengst showed me that the frog was definitely his and I was not going to take it away from him." At one point, Mike, his daughter, and his mom were all fostering puppies at the same time. "Once you become a part of the MWD community, you begin to realize the immense role these animals play in keeping our troops and our

Mike's dog bone–shaped pool is a gathering place for fosters and their warrior pups. PHOTO BY JEFF KAMEN.

law enforcement personnel safe," Mike says. "You also become aware of dogs who perish saving the lives of humans. In the past, I never cried for a dog I did not know. I now grieve when a police dog gets shot, when a MWD triggers an IED and perishes, or when a dog gives his life to save a human being."

CHAPTER 12

PPATRIOT AND HIS MOMMY

It's a typical pre-dawn morning in the Guard Mount room at the Dog Training School. PPatriot, an outrageously cute eight-week-old Breeding Program puppy, is sitting on foster mom Stephanie P.'s lap. In almost any other male-dominated setting, Stephanie would be getting all the attention, but this puppy is *really* cute, and all the trainers are serious dog lovers. Some of them stretch out their hands to lure PPatriot from Stephanie. The Belgian Malinois pup is happy to oblige but after the first three licks of your finger, expect a bite and a shake of his head. He may be a baby, but he's also a predator. Because it's Lackland K9, biting is not discouraged. Having a serious bite drive is important for a Military Working Dog. Soon enough, trainers will begin getting PPatriot's biting under control.

At the end of Guard Mount, Stephanie is called into her civilian boss's office and gets a surprise. John M. (aka "Papa Bear"), a veteran US Army dog handler and now course chief at DTS, tells her, "You're doing great! I'm giving you command of your first trailer, beginning today. You've got Team 9!"

The trailers that ferry warrior pups from the kennels to the training areas contain individual, air-conditioned cabins for eighteen dogs. If you're a trainer, being assigned your own trailer means you are responsible for getting those puppies graduated from basic training in 120 working days. With this responsibility comes supervisory command over a team of about five trainers from all the military services.

PPatriot is expected to become a bomb-sniffing, ambush-hunting war dog. Just not yet. PHOTO BY JEFF KAMEN.

DTS course chief "Papa Bear" and lead instructor Stephanie P. holding her foster PPatriot. PHOTO BY JEFF KAMEN.

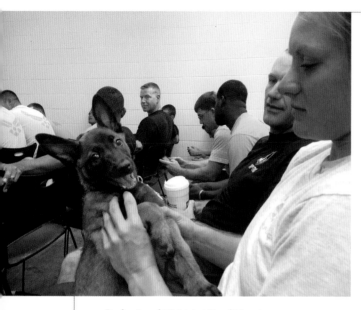

Stephanie and PPatriot at Guard Mount. PHOTO BY JEFF KAMEN.

Stephanie says, "Thank you!" as she beams at him and gives PPatriot a kiss on the side of his snout. She bounds out of his office with the puppy under her arm like a football. Just down the corridor she opens a door to the Team 9 office where five trainers are getting into their Carhartt coveralls. "Hey, guys, Papa Bear just gave me Team 9! I'll meet you at the kennels. Please start pulling our dogs. I'm dropping off PPatriot. I'll be right with you."

Before she joins her team, she has to put PPatriot in doggy day care a few blocks away at the Breeding Program office. Inside Doc's building, several of his staff react joyfully to PPatriot's arrival. That's because they are all so deeply invested in the success of every pup in the program and because he's a total cutie.

In many cases it is impossible to know early on if a warrior pup is going to fail one of the core requirements and wash out of the Dog Training School when they're between thirteen and nineteen months old. So Stephanie and the seventy-two other trainers must pour tremendous energy into each pup in the hope that every one of them will graduate and "make a dog," even though half of them eventually do wash out.

All of these future MWDs are very strong athletes. They will be taught to control their surging strength, but initially they are quite capable of knocking you down or slamming you into a wall. So Dog Training School instructors need extra muscle power. Most DTS trainers, including Stephanie, hit the gym every morning for two hours, before attending the pre-dawn Guard Mount meeting of the Dog Training School.

When she is home, Stephanie puts PPatriot through hours of play and some very preliminary instruction prescribed by Doc for all fosters. So far, PPatriot has a very short attention span and is interested in chasing anything only for a few seconds at a time. That is not a good sign and could be a problem if he were one of the thirteen-month-old dogs Stephanie trains. Fortunately,

Stephanie and PPatriot in front of a trailer that transports Lackland K9s from the kennels to the training areas.
PHOTO BY JEFF KAMEN.

PPatriot is just a baby, and he's got time to develop his focus and drives. After spending almost half a year as a foster and then another six months in Puppy School, odds are he will be "drivey" enough to enter the Dog Training School. "Making a puppy into a Military Working Dog takes time, dedication, and love," says Stephanie.

Weeks later, Stephanie glows with optimism. Her foster pup is progressing nicely after some one-on-one training with Doc to amplify PPatriot's chase and hold drive. Without this drive, he

MWDs sense Stephanie's loving nature and self-confidence. That makes them want to work for her.
PHOTO BY SENIOR AIRMAN PERRY ASTON.

won't graduate Puppy School and will never see the Dog Training School where his mom is a lead instructor.

"Doc tells me PPatriot's doing a lot better and I see it at home," says Stephanie. "He now chases his ball and stays with it instead of jumping from toy to couch to floor, forgetting about the ball."

It's a credit to Stephanie. Although she has become emotionally involved with her first foster, she has no problem shifting back into her professional perspective when asked if PPatriot will make the grade as a Military Working Dog. "Oh, he's a way crazy dog!" she exclaims. "Lots of good energy. If we continue to bring out his natural drives—and we will—he will be a good dog for the right handler!"

Surprise! Stephanie's foster pup PPatriot bites the author's beard. PHOTO BY LESLIE STONE-KAMEN.

Months later, Stephanie happily reports by phone, "PPatriot is becoming a beast!" (In Lackland K9 parlance, "beast" is a very good thing.) "It looks like he's on his way to being the kind of dog a handler wants to have when everything and everyone depends on you." 🐾

THE REQUIREMENTS

To graduate from DTS, dogs must be able to:

- detect the odor of explosives 95 percent of the time (for those trained on narcotics odors, 90 percent of the time)

- alert on an enemy ambush from 400 feet away

- respond immediately to a handler's order to take down a fleeing person

- continue to work in the presence of gunfire

- defend *without* command if a suspect threatens him or his handler

- stop an attack immediately whenever the handler commands "Out!"

CHAPTER 13

SHARIF

USAF Technical Sergeant Sharif D. is a gentle soul with an easy smile and enormous love—especially for his wife, his unit, and for his Military Working Dog. Sharif is a Security Forces police officer at Lackland. He has a wide range of tools and weapons at his command. His favorite and most versatile is his dog.

On one warm afternoon, his portable radio comes to life. Another cop needs K9 backup at one of the dorms for new airmen taking the Basic Military Training course. When Sharif arrives, the officer who called for help is listening to a distraught mother of one of the recruits. She says she's afraid that her son is being recruited to ISIS by his Muslim girlfriend. She also states that she believes the young woman has sent her son something dangerous in the mail.

Sharif and his dog—trained in patrol and explosives detection—enter the recruit's room and sweep it. The dog finds no bomb, no gun, no ammunition. Sharif, however, finds the suspect package. It's a teenager's memory book containing photos of the recruit and his girlfriend.

It turns out that the boy's mom does not approve of the relationship. She invented the ISIS story hoping it would make the Air Force break up the kids. The woman is escorted off the base.

Preparing to defend Lackland against real terrorists is a major part of Sharif's professional life. On April 8, 2016, the training that he and his dog had undergone was tested in an unexpected way. "I had just dropped the dog off at the kennels after a vet appointment that morning," says Sharif. "As I tried to leave the base, the gate guard told me nobody could leave because Lackland was on lockdown. Shots had just been fired. There was an active shooter on base about a mile from the kennels."

Sharif flipped a U-turn, headed to the kennels, grabbed his dog, and raced to the building. As he arrived at the scene, he asked another officer to be his overwatch—that is, to follow him

"I know I can trust my dog with my life and he knows I've got his back. It's all about love and training," says Sharif D. PHOTO BY USAF STAFF SERGEANT VERNON YOUNG.

into the building with his rifle ready to fire to protect the dog and him. Every second counts with an active shooter. They needed to move fast to save innocent lives. They carefully opened closed doors and let the dog search off leash. "Every insecure room I came to, I took the dog off the leash and gave the command, 'Find 'em!' Sending him into the room means momentarily I can't see him but I am confident he will do what we've trained him to do."

Sharif and OOlaf during a briefing for new fosters. PHOTO BY JEFF KAMEN.

Soon, more Air Force and local police were in the building. Sharif and his dog did as they would in combat, leading the way, checking and clearing every room. There were no new gunshots. They moved quickly, but with caution. The dog and Sharif were running point, hunting for the gunman.

Finally, Sharif and the other officers discovered that the shooter was down by his own hand. They quickly established that this was not a case of terrorism, but a workplace tragedy that took two lives. An employee who was about to be disciplined by a review board had brought two guns into the building and opened fire on his boss, killing him, then turned the weapon on himself, triggering the aftermath of fear and confusion.

The incident taught Sharif that he could trust his dog to follow his orders in a real-world situation. Their training had paid off. When they hit that building, dog and man both knew their jobs and they did them without hesitation, functioning smoothly as a team.

When Sharif graduated from the Handlers' Course, he was assigned MWD OOlaf. This K9 powerhouse is a son of the legendary FFalcor. That made Sharif interested in the Puppy Breeding Program. Nowadays, he drops in and volunteers to foster a warrior pup if he's ever needed.

Sharif is meticulously disciplined when he is at work with his canine partner. But his first experience with his foster pup at home was a lesson in humility. "I didn't really follow the rules that I was supposed to—the ones from foster program orientation," he explains. "About never letting your puppy out of your sight and always assuming he's about to make trouble? Yeah, those. I figured I could kind of just do what I want. I mean, I'm a handler of a big bad dog! This puppy would be easy!"

It wasn't just any super energy puppy that Sharif was assigned to raise. Sharif says Breeding Program chief Doc wanted him to "take on this little dude because he really wasn't a normal puppy from the first moment he came out of his mom."

You've seen the photos of how cuddly these future four-legged heroes are when they're given to their fosters. That was not Sharif's experience. "On the day I got him, he was six weeks old and he wants to fight everything, chase everything, and bite everyone. You try to pick him up and he starts snapping at your hands. Not what you expect. Not a nice cuddly puppy."

WARRIOR COP

Security Forces cops are trained to repel attacks on the base from the outside and to deal with anything that happens inside the wire. For Sharif, that includes a very serious relationship with the weight room. He bench-presses more than 300 pounds. It's not an ego thing. It's part of Sharif's personal strategy, preparing his body, mind, and spirit to meet every emergency that might threaten anyone under his protection.

But Sharif reminded himself: "We're not building pets here so maybe this bitey guy could be trained to become one serious K9. Maybe."

One of the rules Sharif ignored is "Don't let the puppy go outside by himself." It was only for a minute. How much could go wrong? "He tore up the water hose and the roller that the water hose was on. He stripped the bark off the bottom couple of feet of a whole tree. He dragged my grill cover with the grill still attached to it across the deck. This all happened in, like, ninety seconds!"

Sharif will never forget that this puppy chewed up the pillar that supported the back of his porch. "This crazy puppy and a friend's dog were playing around the house. They jumped into the recliner, hitting it full speed, and put a hole in the wall! But I'm cool, right? No big deal," says Sharif. "I put some Spackle on the wall and repainted it. As I was waiting for it to dry, I turn my head and see the puppy *eating the Spackle off the wall!*"

Sharif was talking with another Lackland cop when suddenly his former foster saw him and nearly knocked him over with joy. PHOTO BY JEFF KAMEN.

In a state of panic, Sharif called the emergency vet number at Holland Hospital for MWDs. The vet listened and then said the puppy would be fine because he probably didn't eat enough Spackle to make him sick.

Sharif decided to pay closer attention to the rules, which helped, but there were still challenges. "This puppy would jump up on the kitchen counter to try to get food. I didn't even know he could jump that high!"

Sharif bonding with his MWD partner on their day off.
PHOTO BY JANET DELTUVA.

Five and a half months after Sharif brought home the whacko warrior pup, it was time to return the somewhat calmer dog to the Breeding Program so he could begin his new life in the kennels and Puppy School. Sharif was very relieved to see him go.

Sharif heard from his friends who are training his foster that the former trouble-maker was doing very well. "Going to be one badass Military Working Dog," he says proudly. "I'm happy also that he lives in the kennels. Any place but my house!" 🐾

PRIORITIES

"I love my dog," says Sharif, "but our job is to make sure every human being who is with us goes home to their families alive and hopefully unhurt at the end of the day. People may ask, how could you send your dog someplace knowing he could get hurt? I do it because it's what we have been trained to do. Preserve human life."

CHAPTER 14

MARISSA'S FIGHT

Warfighting comes naturally to Marissa. She is one of those soldiers who is wired to enjoy combat. Marissa loves the physical, mental, and emotional challenges, the responsibility to protect her squad, and the uniquely intense camaraderie that is forged in training and battle.

Marissa says her mom was her first hero, a powerful model of dedication who came from Mexico. "She taught me to work hard and love the United States. Now, I have the privilege of defending this wonderful country."

Marissa suffered a shock when two of her closest friends—Army military police like her—were murdered in Afghanistan by hidden IEDs during separate patrols. One bomb was in an abandoned car; another had been hidden at the side of a road. In each case, the squad was not accompanied by an MWD team. After those losses, Marissa vowed that one day she would go into battle with an explosives-detecting K9 so she could save the lives of other good men and women. That dream came true when she deployed with US Special Forces in Afghanistan. "They relied on my dog and me to keep them safe from bombs and ambushes and that's a huge responsibility. But we did it and that's what counts when lives are at stake."

Following her successful deployment overseas, Marissa is now facing a whole new challenge: working as an instructor at the Dog Training School to train the next generation of MWDs. These

> ### TRAINING BITES!
>
> Every Lackland trainer knows she is going to get bitten on the job. The trick is to keep the bites few in number and not very deep. This requires guts, agility, speed, and experience. Marissa's acquiring the experience; she's already got the rest.

Sergeant Marissa J. is a mix of romantic and warrior. She's a US Army dog handler back from combat in Afghanistan, teaching puppies to protect our troops. FAMILY PHOTO.

CHAPTER 15

WOMEN OF STEEL

Today, more young American women than ever are discovering their inner steel and are becoming Military Working Dog handlers. The young woman on the facing page graduated from the Handlers' Course at Lackland and is now at her home base, building the bond with her dog, doing advanced training, and preparing for her next orders. Meanwhile at Lackland, more women trainers are at work in the Dog Training School. Some of them have risen to become Red Patch master trainers.

With this work comes great sacrifice. The American military K9 community still mourns the loss of Sgt. Zainah Caye Creamer, a twenty-eight-year-old from Texarkana, Arkansas, who was killed in action on January 12, 2011. She loved her job as a handler and the power her dog gave her to safeguard our troops. She was planning to become a massage therapist when she retired from the Army. Her joyful nature and enthusiasm made her very popular at her home base at Fort Belvoir in Virginia. Beneath her radiant smile was courage made of steel. You simply cannot do the job without that kind of core. There is no rotating in and out of the point position when you're the dog handler. You've got to be right there, at the tip of the spear as your squad walks into harm's way.

"It breaks my heart that the only female handler to be killed in action was a friend of mine, but she served her country to the fullest extent," says Sergeant Christopher H., now a senior

> ### WALKING POINT
>
> Walking point has always been considered higher risk, but now terrorist organizations offer cash bounties to their snipers and sappers who succeed in shooting or blowing up our handlers. It's gotten even more perilous to lead the way.

It takes inner steel to be a MWD handler. In combat, you must take the lead since that's where your dog's ears and nose need to be to detect ambushes and hidden IEDs. FAMILY PHOTO.

BEST FRIENDS FOREVER

Our MWD team handlers' emotional connections are first with their dogs and then with other handlers based in the same kennels, and with the worldwide American MWD community that has its roots at Lackland.

A handler and her MWD train to find IEDs.
USMC PHOTO BY CPL. JESSICA ETHERIDGE.

in one spot when she apparently stepped on a hidden pressure plate that exploded the IED, taking her life and wounding her dog.

Creamer's name was immediately etched into American military history as the first female working dog handler killed in action during the Iraq and Afghanistan wars. Her boots had been on the ground for less than three months when her life was taken from her.

When word got back to Fort Belvoir, the community conducted a candlelight vigil and a memorial ceremony. They mounted a bronze plaque on a wall next to the entrance to the Fort Belvoir Kennels, which have been named in her honor. Sergeant Creamer's beloved partner, Military Working Dog Jofa, was present at the ceremony and posed in front of the plaque.

Jofa's wounds from the IED blast were not life threatening, but Creamer's death hurt the dog emotionally, according to Captain Auribrio Fennell, 212th MP Detachment commander, who has long experience observing MWDs. "A dog gets traumatized just as much as a human. You can't see their emotional scars through communication verbally, but dogs do communicate. They get sad; they get depressed. I'm sure anytime he picks up her scent on something he has a flashback."

Joy and pride at Lackland after T. Sgts. Terri M. and Melissa C. received their Red Patch master trainer insignia with Breeding Program foster consultant Renae J. (center), a dog handler who fought courageously in Iraq.
PHOTO BY JEFF KAMEN.

Dogs—especially the MWDs selected and trained by Lackland—are also very resilient. After a short break, Jofa shook it off and went back to work for a new handler.

The way the Army honors Sergeant Creamer's sacrifice signals to young women coming into the ranks of MWD handlers that they will be respected members of an elite and noble community of American warriors who risk their own lives to protect their comrades in arms. 🐾

CHAPTER 16

UNDER WATCHFUL EYES

Whether he's in combat as a dog handler, at Lackland training Military Working Dogs, or instructing the men and women who become handlers, US Navy Master-at-Arms Justin T. keeps a careful watch. Despite the seriousness of his work, Justin has a famous sense of humor. In fact, if smiles came in sizes, his would be extra large like the rest of him. Justin stands out even when he isn't standing up. It's the penetrating blue eyes in his large head that sits atop his battle-hardened 6'5" body. He's lean but he's massive.

Long before he was entrusted with training handlers, Justin had deployed overseas five times, once at sea and four times into battle on the ground in Afghanistan with a Military Working Dog at his side, protecting everyone in the unit to which he was assigned.

Justin came to respect and care deeply about many of the Afghan people, who, he said, "loved that we were there to help, to free them from the Taliban, to build schools, to help them have a life. Many men and tons of kids were obviously happy to have us there. Unlike the Russians, we weren't there as occupiers, but liberators."

What told Justin even more strongly that America was doing the right thing was something totally unexpected. "Afghan Muslim women would see us with our guns and me with a big scary dog and they would still run out of their homes, violating strict cultural taboos, to offer us food and tea. That happened to us a lot. They knew that we were putting our lives on the line to save them and they were grateful."

Justin was so good at his job and responded so well under fire, that he and his K9 partner were awarded a Bronze Star Medal, fighting an enemy that, he warns, is "very intelligent. They're picking up on everything that we do, and they try to counter it. But of course we frustrate them—most of the time."

For this American patriot, it's all about saving the lives of Americans and our coalition battle partners in the war against terrorism. PHOTO BY JEFF KAMEN.

Deployed downrange, MWD handler Justin T. and his partner on a good day very far from Lackland.
FAMILY PHOTO.

Taliban bomb makers try to hide their IEDs in metal, in plastic, or in wood. Regardless, there still has to be a component that actually explodes. "We train our dogs to find the odors of those same explosives, leading us to the hidden bombs. Then our EOD (bomb squad) teams safely disarm or blow them up." That's why Taliban snipers routinely hunt for MWD teams as their first-priority targets. During one of Justin's deployments, an American dog handler was taken out by a Taliban sniper's bullet, and a second handler by an IED. In one of those incidents, the handler's dog was also killed. In another, the dog was wounded but lived to fight another day.

Justin recalled one frightening but exhilarating patrol mission in Kandahar province that serves as testament to the irreplaceable power of MWD teams. "After listening to a lot of briefings and being out on the road with my dog, I decided to boost her training so she could sniff out very minimal amounts of the variety of explosives intel told us we should expect. We did that for about a week and my dog was enjoying the training and getting very good at it. Next thing you know, our Marines are given a mission, so the dog and I go with them, outside the wire, leading the way into an area where intel says there are probably IEDs. But where?"

To Justin, the road ahead looked clear. "I've got really good eyes, but I know that I don't have x-ray vision so I for sure cannot know what's buried under the concrete, in the dirt, in an abandoned car. Where we are headed is an obviously great place for an L-shaped ambush—with us as the targets."

Justin says, "I could feel it coming, but I had to stay calm for lots of reasons. Number one is because I know that my energy flows down the leash into the dog. She was up for the work, but she needed to feel that her boss is rock steady. That's a serious part of the relationship. She does the hard stuff and I make her feel safe. I prayed that I had trained her well enough in the previous days, just in case the trap I expected contained only very small amounts of explosives."

Justin with a student handler. The dog is a training aide, an MWD who helps teach handlers their jobs.
PHOTO BY JEFF KAMEN.

Every Marine walking behind Justin and the dog was counting on them to save their lives. Suddenly, Justin saw that his dog, who was working off-leash, had leaped into a dry ditch next to the road and was alerting. Justin bellowed his warning as all hell broke loose.

"The Taliban's battle plan assumed we would drive right up to their hidden detonator—that we would drive over bomb one, bomb two, bomb three, then bam, bam, bam! There goes the entire convoy. Including the dog and me." But the squad's commander had ordered all of his people to dismount from their vehicles a hundred yards earlier. That meant the dog and handler could do their job which requires them to be on the ground. As is usually the case in real-life combat, what came next happened very fast.

"We were all on foot and headed straight into the invisible Taliban trap when they saw we weren't driving into their plan," Justin explained. "So they opened fire from a position that was far enough away to be out of sight but close enough to be effective—if they hit their targets. Now, while we're taking this fire, my dog just starts going crazy. Not her normal like, 'Oh, man, we're getting shot at,' but more like, 'Hey Justin, I smell something you like me to find! You got my tennis ball?' She just stopped in her tracks and sat there. And I'm like, 'What the heck are you looking at?' All I could see was her staring into space and moving her head from side to side. Bullets are zinging all around us, our guys are pouring rounds into the enemy position, and I climb down into the canal next to my dog. I line up on her nose and look a little bit closer. There it was, almost invisible: a fishing line! That fishing line, which I surely would have missed on my own, was a critical piece of a low-tech but very effective command detonation system that would have allowed the Taliban to trigger the blasts from their hiding place. In the confusion of the firefight, the Taliban must have gotten distracted!" The EOD team raced in behind Justin and cut the fishing line. That made their bombs useless. The Taliban couldn't trigger their IEDs. How did Justin's dog detect the fishing line? "The bomb maker," says Justin, "may have accidentally smeared a very small amount of explosives onto it when he set the trap. My dog alerted on that very tiny amount. Good dog!" And yes, Justin gave him the tennis ball.

Now, seven years later, Justin is still saving American lives, but this time, he's doing it at Lackland. The warehouse-like buildings in which he teaches are packed with boxes, furniture, and racks in rooms that look like offices, bedrooms, and storerooms. It was through the Handlers' Course that Justin learned his trade, being the human half of an MWD team. Now, he's putting brave volunteers from the Army, Navy, Air Force, and Marines through that process. An essential part of his job is scaring the hell out of student handlers so they can survive and succeed in their mission to save American lives the way he did in Afghanistan.

A typical training day goes something like this. A student enters the building, stands at attention, and announces his name, rank, and the name of the dog at his side. The dog and the handler trainee then wait for an order to search a corridor and the rooms that open from it.

Unbeknownst to the student, Justin may have set a harmless but embarrassing booby trap. The student is ordered to begin the search. Considering that this is a simulation of a real-world mission, the student is appropriately fearful that he may miss something. He charges from room to room, letting his dog set the pace, hunting for explosives odor. This could turn into a problem if he lets the dog operate without first doing a visual check before he lets the dog enter each new space. Handlers can spot things dogs can't—like a hanging, sparking electrical cable, broken glass, or a hole in the floor.

Justin speaks at a remembrance ceremony in Sasebo, Japan, for two US Navy Working Dogs. US NAVY PHOTO BY MASS COMMUNICATION SPECIALIST 3RD CLASS KRISTOPHER S. HALEY.

As he races into the last room off the corridor, he is so focused on the dog, he misses a lethal threat that a handler had better see. Suddenly, Justin roars at him with his thundering baritone, "Stop! You got tunnel vision! You were concentrating so hard on reading your dog's reaction, you missed the big box with the words BOOBY TRAP BOMB on it! Because you missed the booby trap, your dog is dead, you are dead, and everyone in the squad walking behind you is dead. You're a good man, and you're gonna be an effective handler, but you gotta pay attention to everything, not just your dog. Got it? Good. Now listen up. Do not tell any of your brothers and sisters out there what to expect in here. If you tell them, you will damage their training! You may tell them it ain't easy and that is all you may say. Clear? Good. Now, get out of here and relax!" Justin gives him a huge smile as the student leaves and another one comes in with his dog.

Justin wants to point out that he has a PTSD service dog, who helps him through rough patches. He encourages all service members who also need help to get it. After all, it's their right. 🐾

CHAPTER 17

MIND READER

This is a story about a Military Working Dog dog named Nido who could read his handler's mind, or so it seemed. But first we must meet the young man who is the human half of Nido's team, USAF Staff Sergeant Devin T.

Devin enlisted right out of high school after a recruiter told him that if he really liked fighting, Uncle Sam would give him a chance to do just that in the defense of our country. "My parents were real good to me," Devin says, "but I was a lousy student and pretty irresponsible. By the time I hit eighteen, I was heading for trouble. I knew I needed a way out of all that nonsense. My body was up for the Basic Military Training course that everyone has to take when they arrive at Lackland, and fortunately, my mind stopped fighting the necessary discipline soon after I arrived."

As he grew to love his new life inside the base, Devin decided he wanted a part in defending it. He applied to be an Air Force cop. Devin turned out to be a natural. Air Force police—officially, Security Forces—are trained to protect everyone and everything on the base against any threat.

Devin heard about the adrenaline-filled adventures that come with being half of an American Military Working Dog team and the respect and prestige that goes with being a K9 handler. He

RESPECT FROM THE ENEMY

Some would-be attackers of US military bases have told police that they ultimately didn't carry out their assault plans because the military police were so alert, well-armed, and clearly prepared to stop anyone who attempted to invade the base. Those bad guys were talking about Security Forces cops like Devin T.

What happens when your dog begins to read your mind?
PHOTO BY SENIOR AIRMAN RACHEL WATSON.

USAF Staff Sergeant Devin T. and MWD Nido. PHOTO BY SENIOR AIRMAN RACHEL WATSON.

knew what his missions could include: protecting the perimeter of Air Force bases at home and abroad, providing bomb detection protection for the president of the United States when he travels, and leading anti-terrorist units into combat anywhere in the world.

Through the tough eleven-week Handlers' Course, Devin learned humility from the combat veterans who taught him the art of being a K9's partner. During one day of training, Devin and an experienced K9 were ordered to find bombs in a plane fuselage. Baits containing the odor of some of the many explosives the dogs are taught to recognize were hidden in and around the seats and overhead compartments.

Devin's part of the job was to lead the dog and make sure that the K9's nose explored every possible hiding place. The dog would do the rest. Their teamwork was solid. The dog alerted on every one of the concealed baits. To a human being they have no odor. To a trained dog, however, the smell is obvious. In basic training, every time an MWD signals he's correctly detected a threat, he gets a reward. But in combat, with bullets flying all around, the reward may have to wait. When Devin saw a busload of new recruits arriving at Lackland one day, he remembered his first day there. "Back then, I thought I knew what I had gotten into, but no matter what the recruiter tells you, the experience is something else!" Eight years after getting off one of those buses, Devin now knows what to expect. Those recruits, he says, "are about to receive an upgrade in body, mind, and spirit from the United States Air Force."

Long before he entered the Handlers' Course, Devin had dramatically changed from the reckless kid he had once been. He had risen in rank to become an Air Force cop, charged with protecting thousands of lives and billions of dollars in planes and other equipment. Now, with the Handlers' Course behind him, Devin was taking on new responsibilities.

During long deployments overseas, the bond between human and K9 becomes even more intense. In some cases, the handler can feel as if the dog is reading his mind and vice versa. One day, Devin had Nido working off-leash, helping to guard a US airbase inside Iraq. The temperature was about 120 degrees and a disturbance was percolating at the entrance to the base.

Devin frames the story this way: "Eager local Iraqi day workers are lined up waiting to be admitted to the base, when a crazy fight breaks out over who will get in first. I wondered whether something should be done to stop it." Right then, and without an order from Devin, MWD Nido

THE UPGRADE BEGINS

Less than twenty-four hours after they arrive at Lackland, new recruits begin Basic Military Training. They learn to follow instructions on how to do everything the Air Force way. That includes how to march while chanting warfighter cadences like this one:

"Hey, I'm a steam roller baby,
Just a'rollin' down the line
So you better get outta my way now
Before I roll right over you!"

Even in battle zones, when you are not actually under fire or about to be, you exercise your dog. Training is a constant in the lives of MWD teams. PHOTO BY SENIOR AIRMAN RACHEL WATSON.

vaults over a concrete barrier and charges the brawling workers. The barrel-chested K9 thunders a sharp warning bark and snaps his teeth at them.

Devin realizes his dog might be about to create an international incident, so he bellows two words: "Nido! Out!" The Mal screeches to a halt, stops barking, and glares at the retreating locals. "Nido! Come!" Although still trembling with adrenaline, Nido leaps back over the barrier and returns to Devin's side, happily wagging his tail. Devin is relieved that his MWD has immediately obeyed the "Out!" command and gives Nido his favorite chew toy before leading him to a nearby air-conditioned shed to cool off. Not realizing the big, scary dog has left the scene, the locals nervously and quietly resume their queue.

Pre-deployment training preps MWD teams for battle. USMC PHOTO BY CPL. AARON DIAMANT.

Devin did well during that deployment. Next, he was sent home for more advanced training. While he was overseas, he learned that his marriage had fallen apart. That was a lot to handle. One night, however, Devin heard news from France that took his mind off his personal life and made him ache to get back into the fight. ISIS terrorists had carried out attacks against innocent, unarmed civilians in Paris. During the police response a French MWD named Diesel was killed as she led the counterattack.

"When we were hit at the Pentagon and the World Trade Center," Devin said, "the people of France declared, 'We are all Americans!' That ISIS attack in Paris made all of us French," said the talented Air Force dog handler, "and murdering Diesel made it even more personal for me. I can only hope MWD Diesel sank her teeth deep into the enemy before she died."

Military Working Dog handler Devin T. has gotten so good at his job, he's been selected to be an instructor at Pre-Deployment Training, the post-graduate school for MWDs and their handlers before they are sent into combat. 🐾

CHAPTER 18

PUPPY IN THE NORTHERN LIGHTS

If you were to drive directly north, about four thousand miles on I-35 from Lackland Air Force Base in San Antonio, you would arrive at the main gate of Eielson Air Force Base in the heart of Alaska. That's where you would find several MWD teams, including OOpal and her handler, USAF Staff Sergeant Mathis W., protecting the almost seven thousand people on the base as well as a vast inventory of extremely valuable aircraft, ammunition, and buildings inside the fence line.

Like Mathis, his faithful K9 partner OOpal is trained and equipped (including dog booties) to withstand temperatures as low as 50 degrees below zero. Together, they face long hours of darkness during the Alaska winter. The strong relationship between dog and handler and the camaraderie of the MWD teams at Eielson help combat the seasonal depression associated with long periods without light near the North Pole.

OOpal's career started at Lackland, where she was born, fostered, and trained. Her lead trainer at the Dog Training School was Technical Sergeant Steve N., a US Air Force cop, dog handler/trainer, and devoted dad. He remembers how unusually aware and caring of humans the sixteen-month-old OOpal was. "She made sure that she did not tear up my hand when we were doing bite work," he says. "You have to expect to get bitten because the dogs are still learning to control their natural

PRESIDENTIAL SUPPORT MISSIONS

Typically, when the president of the United States is scheduled to speak at a major public event, dozens of MWD teams, in coordination with the Secret Service, are required to examine and declare as safe every inch of a huge venue like a sports stadium.

Born in Lackland, on guard in Alaska, OOpal is precious to everyone she protects. USAF PHOTO.

CHAPTER 19

"BEAST"

In Lackland K9 speak, a "beast" describes a pup who has it all—boldness, powerful hunting drive, fierce intelligence, intense determination, and an unstoppable desire to play and learn. MWD EEverest is one of those beasts.

When he was only six weeks old, EEverest was showing clear signs of the fabulous beast he would become. In the facing photo, you'll see EEverest undergoing refresher training designed to help him ignore the distracting sounds of combat when it's his time to lead the way into battle with his handler, who's firing the blank rounds. It's called "gunfire desensitization" and it begins in the Dog Training School at Lackland. The first exposure Lackland Breeding Program dogs are given to the sound of a bullet being fired occurs in a very controlled setting. Because EEverest was born at Lackland, it's easier for him to learn to remain neutral because he's familiar with the sounds of battle.

Long before EEverest entered their lives, his foster family had already adopted two of the program's warrior pups whose unexpectedly submissive personalities had eliminated them from training. Although they were not the original fosters of the dogs, they had decided to give them a forever home when they learned they had washed out of the program. That was years before EEverest came to stay in their house. At least they thought it was their house.

"When EEverest arrived, we decided to bring him out of his crate for a quick meet and greet with our big dogs," foster mom Sandy H. reminisces. "I asked my daughter Ashley to hold their leashes tightly and not let them get too close to the baby. I was thinking our two guys might startle tiny EEverest."

Sandy then reached into the crate and put a leash on EEverest. She gently led him out of the crate. What happened next startled everyone. "Little EEverest took off after my two big dogs in a flash! It wasn't our new baby who needed protecting, it was our two grown up mild Mals! From that

MWD EEverest going through gunfire desensitization training. PHOTO BY HEATHER JUDKINS.

BIG BITE

A mature Belgian Malinois has a bite pressure of as much as fourteen hundred pounds per square inch. That is more than enough to do real damage if the dog gets the right grip and then holds. If he doesn't have a solid bite, he could potentially lose some teeth in the struggle as well as lose the bad guy who he's holding for his handler to arrest.

first day everybody knew that EEverest was the alpha dog! And he was not even six weeks old!"

EEverest was the first puppy that Sandy and her family had ever fostered. "Wow, what a learning curve!" she exclaims. "My grandmother called him 'Hell on Wheels.' Thankfully, the Breeding Program's foster coordinator, Tracy, was knowledgeable, supportive, and available. But even she admitted that EEverest was a challenging case. He was in a class by himself when it came to his focus, strength, and inquisitiveness. And of course, he was just a baby, so he had not yet learned anything about controlling his impulses."

It became clear that the new puppy was not going to be a good fit with the house dogs, so Sandy kept them apart while making sure they all got the attention and exercise they needed. For EEverest, that included long, happy hours of ball chasing. "Having EEverest was one of the best workout programs ever. He never got tired of playing ball. Like everything else he did, his ball drive was on max. I always gave up throwing the ball long before he had enough," says Sandy.

If helping EEverest build on his ball drive was a challenge for his foster family, supporting his preliminary nose work was probably the easiest job they had with him. "We could just throw handfuls of Cheerios around the yard," Sandy said, "and he would use his nose to find and eat them. Another fun chore was taking him into town to outdoor bars and restaurants to socialize him. He needed to be exposed to as many different people and situations as possible." Of course, they had to keep their eyes glued on him.

At home, Sandy would sit him in the corner of the kitchen so he could see her from his crate while she cooked or washed dishes. "He was always so alert and watched everything I did with obvious focus," Sandy says.

At first, Sandy would put EEverest on a long leash and take him for a walk in their front yard. "He'd just be walking along, more like bounding along, when a stray weed or tall piece of grass

EEverest and his foster mom Sandy H. FAMILY PHOTO.

would catch his attention. Well, then it was on! He'd start running and then he'd pounce! Then he'd bite a weed and shake his head to make sure it was still in his grasp," Sandy says. By the end of the day, Sandy felt as if her arm had been pulled from its shoulder socket. She decided it would be better to have the leash halfway up her shoulder and wrapped twice around her arm to make sure she could keep EEverest under control. "There was just no casually holding the leash in my

As early as six weeks old, EEverest was already showing signs of being a "beast." FAMILY PHOTO.

hand and taking a stroll with this guy," Sandy recalls. "I pretty much had permanent bruises on my arms from our walks."

Sandy and her family followed Doc's detailed instructions in the Foster Manual. Accordingly, they put EEverest through his preliminary bite work. The bite training involves teaching the puppy to properly bite on a towel using his full mouth. "I would push the towel all the way to the back of his mouth and then tug on it," Sandy says. This was so he would not bite with just his front

WARRIOR PUPS

teeth, but with his full mouth, bringing the full pressure of his jaws to the task. "Knowing that part of his future job could be biting bad guys on command, EEverest needed to know how to get a secure bite and hold it until instructed to release," she explains.

"When he was a baby, it was fun to play with the bite towels," Sandy remembers. "But as he grew and got a lot stronger we had to wear thick leather gloves to avoid getting bitten while we were doing the same exercises. EEverest would lunge and snap his jaws really hard as he went after the towels."

He was by far the most work and the most difficult puppy that Sandy and her husband have fostered. "All the things that made EEverest a handful are also the traits that make for the perfect working dog," says his foster mom.

MWD EEverest turns out to have been well named. In Puppy School and then in the Dog Training School, the pup with tons of attitude was at the top of his class in controlled aggression and in the detection of explosives. Once his nose locates a trained odor, EEverest absolutely locks onto it, pointing to it until his handler acknowledges the find and then rewards him for it. All of that, combined with being steady as gunfire rings out, makes EEverest just the kind of protection our warfighters need. 🐾

LEARNING TO IGNORE GUNFIRE

At Lackland, a fifteen-month-old dog is first introduced to gunfire while he's having a great time chasing a ball thrown by his trainer. At first, shots are fired from a hundred yards away while the dog is chasing the ball. Gradually, the gun is shot closer and closer until it's being fired by the handler next to the dog, who is happily concentrating on the ball.

CHAPTER 20

LOVE AND SCIENCE

Like their human handlers, when American war dogs get banged up in training or in combat, they receive a full range of medical attention so they can regain their strength and get back to the jobs and the people they love.

For MWDs, as with the soldiers they protect in battle, there are some wounds that go deeper and cannot be seen on the most advanced x-ray machines. Treating these wounds can require specialized expertise.

At any moment, a request for help can come into Lackland from anywhere our forces are deployed. It is the kind of phone call no one wants to get about a loved one in deep pain who is not responding to standard treatment. The voice on the other end of the long-distance call may be coming from a worried American military doctor who's highly skilled and experienced, but, like her colleagues, feels stumped. She doesn't know what to do for the heroic patient in her care, half a world away from his home in San Antonio. This patient might be a five-year-old Military Working Dog. He has no serious physical wounds, but he has stopped working for his handler. Previously a high-energy powerhouse, he now barely responds to any stimulus. He seems withdrawn. This

CANINE PTSD

To properly treat canine PTSD is challenging, Dr. B. says, "because with canines experiencing stress, you cannot ask them to just tell you what happened, to describe their feelings." Under Dr. B.'s direction, US military veterinarians stationed around the world who call for help often experience considerable success, even though their patients refuse to talk about their problems—even for a cookie.

Kris R., a Lackland veterinary technician, is part of the team that embodies love and science at Holland Memorial Hospital for MWDs. PHOTO BY JEFF KAMEN.

Dr. Walter B. at Holland Hospital.
PHOTO BY JEFF KAMEN.

densely muscled, highly intelligent war dog is experiencing what seem to be psychological problems following exposure to the sounds, smells, and sights of battle.

On the other end of the call, in an office at Holland Hospital for Military Working Dogs, the world's leading authority on canine post-traumatic stress disorder listens carefully and then offers advice. It's an important part of what Dr. Walter B., DVM, does as the chief of Behavioral Medicine. Often, this very wise specialist is able to help the veterinarian on the other end of the call fully restore the dog's confidence and sense of well-being. The process can take months. But it pays off when the dog is able to return to duty and the life of action and service that he loves.

The hospital is a hopping place. Hundreds of dogs arrive and leave from here every year. Some need high-tech medicine. Others have recovered from specialized surgery and are well enough to return to their units around the world.

Every three months, as many as 110 young dogs are flown in from Europe where they have been purchased from traditional breeders through dog brokers in Amsterdam. They, too, will enter the Dog Training School. All of those pups must undergo quarantine to make sure they are healthy and to prevent the spread of diseases to other Lackland dogs.

Each warrior pup is a potential future military hero, a defender of our troops, and a saver of lives. Every single one of them is treated with deep love and respect. This is reflected in the quality of their veterinary care. Spend some time with the staff at Holland and what you see is a passion for

READY FOR ANYTHING

Holland Hospital's professional staff is led by fourteen veterinarians with advanced training in surgery, radiology, internal medicine, critical care, epidemiology, physical therapy, and animal behavior. There are six administrative support personnel, a medical laboratory specialist, twenty-four registered veterinary technicians, and animal care specialists.

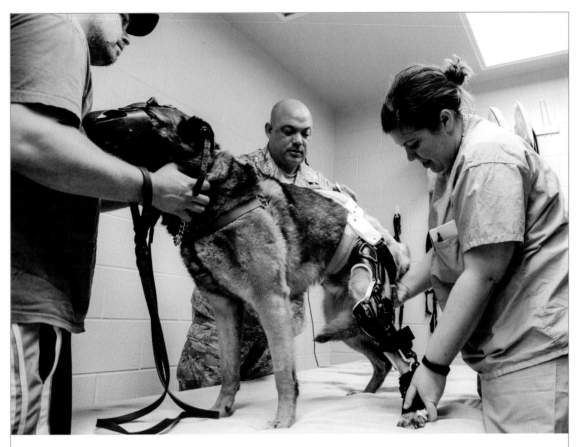

MWD SStash is being fitted for a leg brace to facilitate his healing. All MWDs learn to accept wearing muzzles as puppies, so when necessary—as in medical situations—it is not stressful for them. PHOTO BY STAFF SERGEANT MICHAEL ELLIS, USAF.

understanding, caring, and love that you would wish to see at any hospital, whether for animals or people.

Holland is the only Level 4 veterinary hospital run by the Department of Defense—fully capable of taking on the most difficult challenges on behalf of its patients. It is a one-of-a-kind referral center for the entire US military K9 system. The team at Holland provides primary and specialty level care as well as consultative services, which includes Dr. B.'s expertise on canine PTSD. Holland's resources also support other federal agencies such as the Transportation Security

Outside the hospital, Major Andrea H., DVM, Holland's head of rehabilitation medicine and her team work to help an MWD recover from an injury. PHOTO BY JEFF KAMEN.

Administration (TSA), whose baggage- and passenger-sniffing dogs receive training at Lackland as part of the National Explosives Detection Canine Team Program.

Hospitals in the civilian world are often named for wealthy donors. In the military, they are named for our heroes. Lieutenant Colonel Daniel E. Holland was a brave Army veterinarian who went to Iraq in 2006 to help Iraqi farmers. Dr. Holland was killed by a terrorist IED when it exploded near the vehicle in which he was traveling. Had a Military Working Dog team been assigned to clear that area of hidden bombs earlier that same day, the IED might have been discovered and defused, sparing Holland's life. Today, his name lives on in honor at the only US hospital dedicated to our Military Working Dogs.

Vet Tech Kris R. is honored to work at the hospital bearing Dr. Holland's name. "I've been working here for fourteen years, and I just love it!" she says. "I'm assigned to the care and breeding

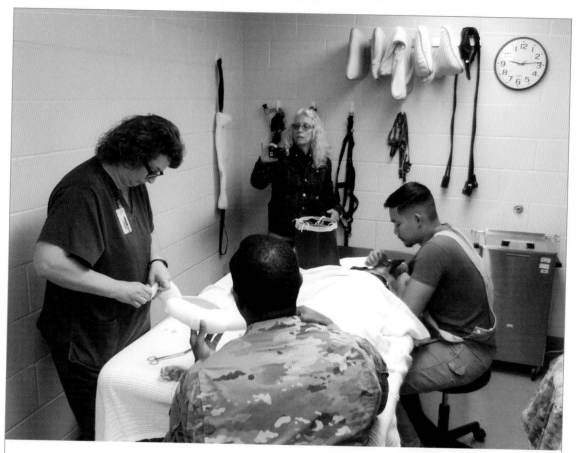

Leslie photographs as an MWD's wounded leg is bandaged while a handler strokes the dog's face at Holland Hospital.
PHOTO BY JEFF KAMEN.

of the adult dogs in the Breeding Program. I actually wound up adopting a retired Military Working Dog who I had fostered when he was just a baby. The day he came home with me for the rest of his life was my best day ever!" 🐾

CHAPTER 21

FULL CIRCLE

Nothing can fully prepare you for how deeply you will fall in love with your first foster puppy from the Defense Department's Military Working Dog Breeding Program. Lisa and Jerry N. found out the only way you can—by diving in. They wanted to do whatever they could to help protect US and allied troops. Fostering a warrior pup seemed like a perfect way to step up. Little did they know that they were about to become part of something way bigger than themselves.

When they receive their call to pick up their foster pup, Lisa and Jerry are thrilled. They know it would be challenging but very rewarding—if everything goes just right. "Jerry and I work hard at what we take on," Lisa proclaims. "We're ready."

Lackland is a short ride from their home. Jerry is active duty so they do not have to go through the security check required of civilians. They follow directions for about three-quarters of a mile on a winding two-lane road to a very ordinary-looking building with no sign on the door.

> ### FOSTERING A FUTURE K9 HERO
>
> **Many San Antonio area families apply for the privilege of fostering, but only one hundred families are selected each year. After all, it's not just a puppy they are asking to raise. It's half of a life-saving defensive weapon system.**

As soon as Jerry and Lisa walk inside, their eyes are drawn to a large photo of a formidable Belgian Malinois with her fangs flashing as she strains against her handler's leash during a controlled-aggression training exercise. *Wow!* Lisa thinks as she looks at the photo, *I hope our foster puppy grows up to be a fierce defender of our soldiers like that one!*

Baby PPershing at the US Military Working Dog Teams National Monument, Lackland AFB. FAMILY PHOTO.

Lisa holds her new foster pup. PHOTO BY JANET DELTUVA.

Lisa, Jerry, and the other fosters are ushered into the training room where they listen to a briefing on the joys and pitfalls of fostering. It's filled with cautionary stories of "wicked smart" athletic puppies that tear into anything while charming everyone in sight. At one point, the speaker holds up what had been brake lines for a one-ton truck. They had been totally ripped up in a matter of seconds by a single foster pup—while they were still installed in the truck! There are good reasons why experienced fosters refer to their truly fierce little canines as "malociraptors," "malligators," and "fur missiles."

Jerry and Lisa pay close attention to the long list of dos and don'ts. They had done considerable reading about Belgian Malinois dogs and knew a lot about what they were getting into. *Okay,* Jerry thinks, *let's meet our baby dog!*

A moment later, three Puppy Program staffers stride into the room, each bearing a little bundle of wriggling joy. One of them walks up to Lisa, carefully hands her a baby dog and says, "Here's your foster puppy. His name is PPershing. Good luck!" Lisa's heart leaps as she cradles the pup. Jerry throws his arms around his wife and the tiny PPershing.

On the way home, Lisa, Jerry, and PPershing stop at the US Military Working Dog Teams National Monument at Lackland. The monument was created by John Burnam, a heroic US Army Vietnam War canine handler, author, and retired master sergeant. Jerry and Lisa follow foster tradition by reverently posing PPershing inside the monument's helmet. At first, the little warrior pup seems worried, but then, he looks more confident.

For the next five and a half months, Lisa and Jerry follow the detailed instructions contained in the Puppy Program's Foster Manual. There are hard and fast rules for feeding, teaching basic obedience, socializing the dogs in all kinds of public settings, and daily exercise. "A well-exercised puppy is a happy puppy! At least four hours a day of vigorous physical activity, play, and training, spaced out in small intervals, is ideal," the manual directs.

It's a lot of intense hard work and outrageous fun. Because of their efforts and his genetics, PPershing grows into one very confident young

Quite grown up PPershing poses outside Lisa and Jerry's home. FAMILY PHOTO.

dog. In the blink of an eye, the almost six months of fostering is over, and Lisa and Jerry have returned to Lackland with PPershing. They've parked the car and gotten PPershing out of his car crate, hooked up his leash, and walked into Holland Hospital. But this time, it isn't for the regular monthly training session with the other fosters or the routine weigh-in and health check.

Jerry and Lisa take seats in the waiting area. PPershing sits next to Lisa. This is the point at which some fosters secretly hope their baby washes out of the program in a few weeks and they get to take him home with them forever. It's widely known among fosters that some pups simply do not adapt well to their new life back on the base and some of those dogs do get sent home to their fosters permanently.

NOT YOUR AVERAGE DOGS

Some first-time foster parents have big hearts and great intentions, but cannot withstand the actual, sometimes seemingly endless demands for patience, time, and energy that go into raising these warrior pups. In those cases, the frustrated first-timers return the puppy to the Breeding Program, which quickly places the baby MWD-to-be into another foster home.

Lisa and Jerry know they might never again see the dog they have come to love so much. They've been briefed on exactly what will happen next. They have known this was coming for almost six months but now it's real. The three of them wait to be taken into the clinic for PPershing's final foster health check. Lisa and Jerry are doing their best to keep it together emotionally. They haven't been in the hospital for more than a few minutes when another couple enters and sits nearby.

Jerry smiles and tells them about PPershing, that they are about to turn him in to begin his formal military training. The other couple starts telling Lisa and Jerry that they have come to pick up a ten-year-old MWD who's just been retired. They're going to take him home and share their life with him.

For Lisa it's an almost overwhelming moment. "Here we are just about to turn in our baby to start his career, and there they are, picking up a veteran MWD to give him a comfy retirement—in their home, in their arms. Full circle of life I guess."

Moments later, the quiet drama of their farewell begins to unfold just as Lisa and Jerry were told it would. Tracy, the foster consultant, arrives at the appointed time. Tracy gently leads PPershing and his family from the waiting area about thirty feet down the corridor, through the secured double doors and into a veterinary treatment room.

A US Army vet tech is waiting with a calm smile. She's been through this moment dozens of times and understands how powerful it is for the family. She examines the puppy, says how good and strong PPershing looks and what a good job Lisa and Jerry have done. When the brief exam is over, Tracy says, "It's time." Lisa hugs PPershing and begins to break down. Tracy guides the dog out the side door, and PPershing marches alongside her out of the hospital with his tail held high, on his way to his new life in the kennels and a year of basic training. He never looks back.

Lisa is crying softly. Jerry is clutching her and the empty leash as they head for the exit that takes them back through the waiting room. There they see the other couple having just been handed their newly retired war dog. He's a beauty with a little gray in his cheeks.

The couple waves them over and motions them to join them. The old MWD sees them coming and somehow knows exactly what to do. He slowly approaches. Lisa leans forward to pet him. He leans into her and then looks into her eyes and licks away her tears. In that moment Lisa knows that if PPershing adjusts well to the kennels and goes on to have a career protecting our military, she and Jerry will probably want to adopt an old, retired Military Working Dog and bring him to his forever home—with them. 🐾

Lisa says farewell to PPershing.
PHOTO COURTESY LISA AND JERRY N.

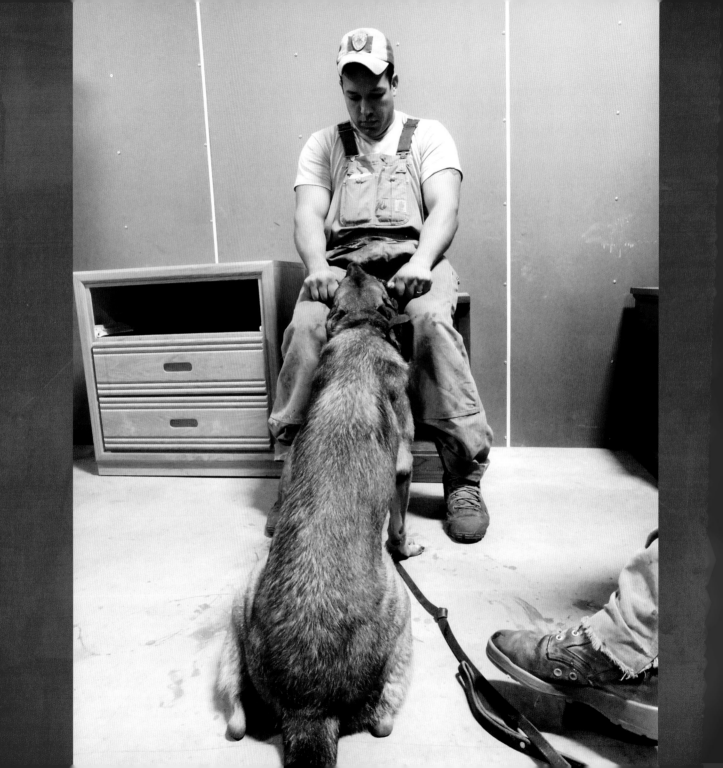

CHAPTER 22

RED PATCH BOBBY

USAF T. Sgt. Bobby V. is one of those people who keeps his mouth shut until he has something to say. His eyes take in everything. Bobby, a US Air Force master sergeant, doesn't miss a chance to find a teachable moment as his team moves each K9 through its training. His concentration is unyielding. Maybe it's all that time in combat—more than a hundred patrols with his MWD partner, or that long period when he led a Security Forces team guarding nuclear weapons. Bobby has the Lackland Magic. He's a master trainer. The Red Patch that's stitched onto his government-issued coveralls proclaims it.

It's just after 0630 hours, and the warrior pups in Lackland's kennels are excitedly anticipating the arrival of the trainers. They know the sounds of their truck-drawn trailers and the scents of the trainers themselves. The dogs love the sounds and those scents because they mean that they are about to have fun. For the dogs, training is all about play.

Bobby strides into a long kennel building, leash in hand. Seventy other trainers are on the same mission: to get the pups they are scheduled to train that day.

The MWDs come bursting out of their kennels. The combined noise of their excitement is deafening! The dogs and their trainers are all moving in an agile, high-energy dance. If you don't know the steps, it's a whole lot smarter to hang back, far back, and watch. There is no room for incompetent third persons getting in the way.

When Bobby and his team pull dogs from the kennels or work them in the exercise yards or inside the warehouses or airplane fuselages, they have to make sure each dog knows who is leading—and it cannot be the dog. The trainers must radiate self-confidence, have a reliably loving, calm demeanor, and be firm but never harsh. Like anyone, Bobby has his moments of frustration with the job, but never with the goal. He's a combat veteran with a big heart, a ripped upper body, a rapid-processing brain, and a very slow fuse. He needs all of that to do his job.

Red Patch Bobby V. is a master at teaching dogs to trust and so much more. PHOTO BY JEFF KAMEN.

HOW TO IMPROVE TRAINING

Red Patch Master Trainers like Bobby are highly esteemed by the officers who command the 341st Training Squadron. When Major Garon S. took over the unit and wanted to help his people communicate better, he asked Bobby's advice. Bobby said, "Have joint training days so the most experienced instructors from all teams can share their favorite techniques." It worked. Training improved.

"Training these dogs demands paying attention to a lot of moving parts at every moment," he says as he supervises another session of carefully planned instruction for sixteen-month-old canines. These dogs are halfway through their 120-day curriculum. "From the first second you pull a K9 from his kennel, through every moment of the day's training to that last second when you put him safely back into his kennel, you have got to be on the ball, fully focused and really awake. It's a lot of stress because we've got to get this stuff right. We are responsible for creating the foundational learning of every one of these dogs. If we get it right, the men and women responsible for advanced training will have a much easier time preparing these dogs for actual battle."

In one exercise, warrior pups are being taught to reliably alert on the odor of dynamite—a common element in IEDs. When a dog alerts on the odor by jumping up and pawing at the drawer in which the bait with the dynamite is hidden, a lot happens fast. One of the trainers immediately "pays" the pup by throwing the dog's favorite toy in front of him. The dog dives at the toy. His jaws snap shut on it. At the same time, all the trainers in the small room whoop for joy in the high-pitched voices the dogs love to hear. The young dog gets to chew on his most beloved toy. But only for a minute.

Then, the trainers take it away from the pup. That builds up the dog's natural prey drive to grab and then hold what it wants. When you watch working dog demonstrations, you always see the dogs staring at the handler's face with focused intensity. What you're not seeing is that during training the handler has placed the beloved tennis ball or Kong toy in his armpit, and the puppy is fixated on that desired object. That is how the dog learns to stay focused on his handler.

Being a Dog Training School instructor is a challenge to the body as well as the mind and spirit. Even a thirteen-month-old "green" dog is so powerful he can smash you to the ground in an instant. These dogs aren't being mean. They just play hard.

Here, Bobby offers guidance to young instructors on the subtleties of keeping a young dog focused on the odor they want him to detect and alert on. PHOTO BY JEFF KAMEN.

Bobby explains, "These dogs tear you up. It's just what they do. I go to the gym a lot. It's a help. But it's still not enough. I'm in physical pain a lot of the time. We do whatever we can to not get re-injured. You re-injure the same spot, the pain gets even worse."

First as a handler in combat, then as a trainer whose remarkable skills, discipline, and intuition marked him for leadership inside the elite universe of DTS trainers, Bobby has learned to have enormous respect for the dogs. "Once they graduate our basic course and get their first handler, they have to go through a lot," he says. "I've seen dogs switch handlers as much as twelve times in their careers," which can last a decade. "So these dogs have to adapt to new people all the time. It's quite difficult for a dog to do that," says the Red Patch trainer, "but our dogs do perform very well. That high adaptability comes from everything we do. That includes careful breeding, the very careful way we train them, and all the follow-up training and care they get from their handlers after they graduate here and go off to the world out there, beyond Lackland."

Red Patch Bobby and his boss observe the joint teams training that Bobby proposed to improve results.
PHOTO BY JEFF KAMEN.

Bobby keeps his eyes on his training team as they walk dog after dog through the same detection scenario. "You know, handlers are human and that's great but not at every moment. So, part of what we train into the dogs is a kind of backup system against predictable human error."

In Bobby's world, an error can be fatal. "If the dog alerts on trouble and the handler misses that alert because there are distractions like gunfire, explosions or people screaming, an IED can be missed. Then it's triggered and we've got more dead and wounded Americans."

That kind of preventable loss of life, limb, and sanity haunts Bobby. He's not a dramatic guy, but his young face reflects the enormous responsibility he carries into every single day working these dogs. "In reality, a handler isn't always able to be fully focused on his dog," Bobby says. "The handler can miss a cue. And it can be something as small as a change in leash tension—meaning the dog is responding to something. If he does realize his dog is pulling in a new direction or has slowed down, the handler has to take his eyes off the overall situation to put his eyes on his dog."

Bobby says a handler can miss a slight change in leash tension if "he's not feeling well-protected by his security team, or because he's worrying about getting shot and his eyes are sighting down the barrel of his gun."

Bobby has a humble, self-deprecating sense of humor, but there's no mirth in his eyes when he says, "You know we don't employ any superheroes here. But the truth is that this work demands a scary kind of perfection from handlers. It's just the way it is. Of course, some handlers are prone to making mistakes and we may never know that, because in combat they have to operate mostly by themselves with their dog. My job is to help train each dog to be as close as possible to foolproof in that kind of situation."

PAY ATTENTION!

A handler must watch for every subtle change in the dog's body language, which could be a signal that the squad is about to walk into a lethal trap—an IED blast or an ambush.

How does he make this happen? "We do it by building the dog's confidence by making him really good at finding what we want him to find, by learning to alert on it in a way that quickly gets his handler's attention," Bobby explains. "We teach him to be bold and confident about sticking to his find, until his handler pays him for it. If the dog is in full, clear alert and sticking to it, that forces the handler to think about what is going on and to act on it, fast!"

This may sound simple, but consider all of the moving parts. First, a dog has to be trained to signal very clearly when it identifies an odor. That means instead of a mild change in leash tension, that dog—if it's trained right—will stare with its nose pointed directly at the source and sit. He won't move until his handler releases him. That instantly forces the handler's full attention on his dog. In a flash, the handler will yell at the troops walking behind him, "Heads up! My dog's alerting!"

Long before a Military Working Dog is ready for action, the fundamentals must become ingrained. That requires enormous concentration and loving patience by the trainers. One of the most important commands that Bobby and his team must teach the dogs is to immediately stop biting when the trainer says, "Out!" It's an absolute requirement and teaching it successfully can be a long process. It can take many weeks, depending on the dog.

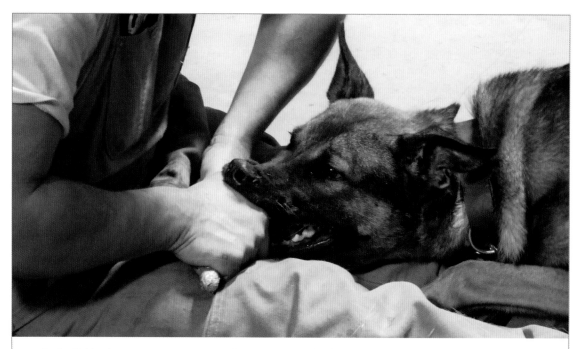

It takes Bobby almost twenty minutes to wear down the young Mal. He's teaching the dog that he will get what he wants by trusting his trainers. PHOTO BY JEFF KAMEN.

At one training session, Bobby is working with a dog who is being especially resistant to obeying the "Out!" command. Bobby is ready for him. He's using a thick black Kong toy with a metal pipe threaded through its middle. This allows enough room for him to put his hands on either side of the toy. The highly determined seventy-pound Mal seizes the Kong and is committed to not letting go.

Bobby's unprotected skin is less than an inch from the clenching teeth of the dog. The Red Patch trainer believes the dog only wants the Kong and has no desire to hurt him. Bobby has to get the dog to release the chew toy and he does it by facing the dog and holding tight. For nineteen seemingly endless minutes, Bobby uses his back, legs, and upper body to wear down the young Mal. Each time the dog releases its grip even a tiny bit, Bobby relaxes a little bit, giving the Kong back to him to increase the dog's awareness that if he will "Out!" he will still receive the coveted toy.

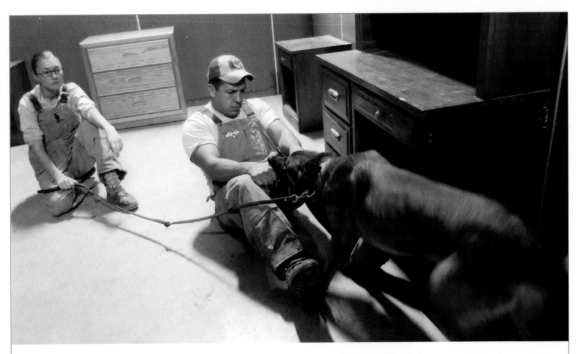

PHOTO BY JEFF KAMEN.

Bobby and his team do this kind of exercise, in varying degrees, day in and day out to teach the dogs that they can get what they want by trusting their trainers and doing what they are told to do. When the pups graduate DTS, that trust is then transferred to their first handlers, with whom they will become a unified MWD team. Bobby knows how that must go because he's already done it. He may never meet those handlers face-to-face, but he feels an enormous personal responsibility to them, and he takes it seriously day after day. 🐾

STOP YOUR ATTACK!

Breeding Program puppies quickly learn the "Out!" command because releasing has been part of their fostering and Puppy School experiences. Baby pups are rewarded immediately for trusting and letting go, knowing they'll get it back.

CHAPTER 23

TRAILBLAZER

At a huge air show inside Randolph Air Force Base in San Antonio, Sarah R. is stretching on tiptoes, at the front of the crowd, to see her husband Ryan, a handsome US Army K9 handler and master dog trainer, prepare to take center stage. It's a performance that displays the power and grace of American Military Working Dogs. On his leash, he has a sleek Belgian Malinois who wants to play "run, bite, and hold!"

In a few seconds she knows her husband will order the dog to take down a fleeing suspect, in this case, another trainer wearing a heavy, padded bite protection suit, so he'll be fine when it's over.

"What does my husband talk about at home? Working Dogs! Working Dogs! Working Dogs! Sometimes me, but mostly, Working Dogs!" Sarah laughs as she looks toward the fenced-in area where Ryan is about to trigger his dog's sudden charge by shouting, "Get him!" Sarah has seen the demonstration many times but is always up for watching her husband work.

REALITY SINKS IN

From the beginning, master trainers teach the newbies that all the dedication, knowledge, and training they put into each dog will one day save someone's life. What made it all click for Ryan was the first time he heard "Hey man. Great job on my beast! He loves to work!" via Facebook from a soldier in the Middle East working with a dog he had trained at Lackland. And that, says Ryan, "feels fantastic."

Between patrols in South Korea, Staff Sergeant Ryan R., a US Army Dog handler and Red Patch Master Trainer, works with MWD Bolt during controlled aggression training. FAMILY PHOTO.

Back at Lackland, Ryan is about to let his dog bite the "enemy," in this case a close friend and fellow trainer wearing a protective bite suit, during a demonstration. PHOTO BY JEFF KAMEN.

Ryan is twenty-seven years old. He is the youngest person ever to be awarded Lackland's prestigious Master Trainer Red Patch. Even dogs who are problems for some other instructors tend to like working for him. "For me, coming to work at Lackland K9 completely changed my life," says Ryan. He was the "lucky guy," the bright, charming, very focused and determined kid who married Sarah, "the prettiest, smartest, most talented" girl in their Dallas high school. After

Ryan is a natural. He connects easily with the dogs he trains. PHOTO BY JEFF KAMEN.

graduation, Ryan opened a tire shop while Sarah worked as a bank teller. But he wanted adventure and a chance to serve his country, so he and Sarah decided he would try the Army while she kept her job. After Army Basic Training and Military Police school, Ryan was ordered to Lackland.

"I'm part of 31Kilo, a new Army career field that does not require you to have been deployed as a handler before you're allowed to train dogs. So, from the moment I arrive, of course, I have to prove myself to the seventy other trainers," says Ryan. "All of them outrank me and are older than me—some of them a lot older." On top of that, they had all been handlers overseas and in danger before they got the great assignment to DTS that Ryan had just been handed like a gift.

It wasn't personal. Many of the established trainers were unenthusiastic about anyone like him—someone who had never actually deployed with a dog—being shoved into their midst.

The management at the Dog Training School expected that. They knew that a flood of 31Kilo kids would be coming to DTS over the years. They hoped Ryan would be a good trailblazer. It worked. Ryan's very respectful attitude, and the overarching sacred nature of the DTS mission, made short

UNEXPECTED SATISFACTION

One day a new dog arrived from Lackland at the kennel in South Korea where Ryan is now deployed. He immediately recognized it as a dog his team had trained at Lackland. A new handler walked into the kennel and was assigned to that dog. As the new MWD team walked out of the kennel together and into an unpredictable future of enormous responsibility and high risk, Ryan felt satisfied. "Oh yeah, that dog will do his job!"

work of the resentment. Others who followed in Ryan's footsteps from the Army program did not encounter the same resistance at Lackland.

DTS course chief, "Papa Bear" is proud of Ryan. "He's got the talent and the discipline, plus, he has the passion and that piece is crucial to doing this work. The day you come to DTS and it feels like it's any other job, that's the day to tell me you're done. But I'm not worried about Ryan. His passion runs deep."

For Ryan, Papa Bear is "like a father figure to me. He always challenges us to do our best because there is so much on the line—the lives of our people."

At one point early in his first year at DTS, Ryan discovered that Papa Bear had ordered four master trainers to see what Ryan was made of— to push him. One of them even brought bagpipes and played loudly during training exercises. "It's his way of forcing you to focus, to concentrate," Ryan says of his mentor. What impressed this young handler most was the reverence the Red Patches brought to their work. "They put so much time, effort, love, and care into these dogs! From the start of my career I wanted to be like them and to live up to their super high standards."

For Ryan, the scariest moment of his career came when he was given command of his own trailer full of eighteen warrior pups and a team of trainers. He had less than six months to turn those thirteen-month-old puppies into war dogs, and he was the kid on the team.

"All eyes were on me. Can a lowly private new to the program cut it? For me, that was scary," Ryan remembers as though it was yesterday. "I didn't want to let down my team and the people in charge who had put me in that position."

Ryan didn't know it, but there was no need to worry. Despite their initial wariness of the new kid, DTS trainers have a strong tradition of supporting each other. So, DTS Team 5, now led by

Ryan, synced quickly with its new boss and produced striking success with its very first trailer of dogs. "We worked our tails off day in and day out to do what a lot of people couldn't. We got into a sweet training zone. We're allowed up to 120 working days to get our dogs certified in basic patrol and odor detection. But, we certified half our dogs in only 102 days and the other nine dogs just one week later in 109 days!"

From then on, says Ryan, "We were a little powerhouse of trainers." For Ryan, it all felt like a blessing. "I wanted a chance to do something important with my life, and the Army gave me Dog Training School. This place is like a dream, filled with smart, tough, funny, hard working men and women who are all on the same mission: to save lives," says Ryan. "I know that any day or night, somewhere in the world, the dogs we trained are on patrol and every one of them has a little piece of my heart."

Eventually, the day came Ryan and Sarah had long expected: orders for his first deployment as a handler to South Korea, seven thousand miles away from their home on the base. Ryan did not want to leave his wife for a year, nor did he want to exchange the warmth of San Antonio for the cold of the Korean winter, but orders are orders.

Soon after Ryan and his dog were acclimated to South Korea, they began patrolling near the demilitarized zone (DMZ) that divides the democratic South from the Communist North. On the

When he's at Lackland, Ryan trains war dogs all day and comes home to his wife and their two house dogs. Pugs, of course. PHOTO BY JEFF KAMEN.

other side of this zone and just out of view, North Korea has arrayed so many large artillery pieces and rocket launchers, it's been estimated that without resorting to its nuclear weapons, the Communist dictatorship could do horrific damage to Seoul, the capital, in just minutes. Once, on his day off while wearing civilian clothes, Ryan went to the public viewing area of the DMZ and peered through powerful binoculars into the far distance. The enemy, he says, is there in large numbers waiting for an order to open fire or to send infiltration teams into the South. "That would be a mistake," says Ryan, "but if they try sneaking into our base, my dog and I and the other K9 teams are ready to give them the appropriate Texas greeting."

Tensions with North Korea have escalated, but Ryan is now safely home in the US. 🐾

CHAPTER 24

SPECIAL OPERATOR

The Puppy School at Lackland is staffed by real people with such strong, colorful personalities they can seem like they stepped out of an action-adventure movie. Like all of them, US Army Special Operator Master Sergeant Clay J. adores puppies.

Not surprising for a special ops warrior, he's into martial arts, and skydiving. He's also an American commando—a highly trained anti-terrorist, whose favorite weapon is his Military Working Dog.

Clay moves with speed, agility, and mindfulness as a fifty-five-pound Malinois pup's flashing teeth tear at his protected left arm during a controlled aggression exercise. When the future MWD responds immediately to the "Out!" command, Clay rewards him with loud praise, the dog's favorite chew toy, and an affectionate hug. The pup leans into him, asking for more. A little more loving follows, but Clay has to move on to the next warrior pup on his list.

Back home in rural upstate New York, Clay was always a little bit faster in body and mind than the other kids. He grew up on stories about great men like his grandfather and sixteen million other American soldiers, sailors, airmen, and marines, who liberated the world from the tyranny of Imperial Japan and Nazi Germany during World War II. Clay was especially drawn to the stories of American commandoes and wondered if he had the guts, physical strength, and brains necessary to be that kind of soldier. Eventually, the US Army would give him the chance to find out, and he seized it with both fists. He ate up all the training the Army offered him and by the time the US invaded Iraq, he was a Special Operations dog handler.

That means he was responsible for the safety of everyone on his team every time they went outside the wire. After all, only his dog—with Clay as interpreter—could detect hidden threats including roadside bombs and enemy fighters hiding in ambush nearby. He was well prepared for this enormous responsibility.

Now training dogs at Lackland, Clay J. was a Special Operations dog handler in Iraq. PHOTO COURTESY CLAY J.

LEARNING THE DOG

"Every last little tilt of his head, positioning of his nose, the set of his tail, the way he moves when he's suddenly alerting on an odor, which could be the bomb that can kill you all— you pay very, very, very close attention to your dog," says Clay.

Almost everyone who volunteers for K9 begins their training where Clay did—at Lackland. "This," he says, "is where you start learning your trade. It takes you almost three months of very hard, sometimes scary work. You graduate Handlers' Course. They ship you out to a kennel at a base somewhere usually in the US and you work with your dog every day. Then, it's pre-deployment where they ramp you up for actual combat. Then you get deployed overseas somewhere and you train your dog to adapt to the local environment. That continues until one day your kennel master says, 'Hey! You're up!' Then, you meet the unit you're gonna walk in front of. They're Americans or allies, but they are strangers. They don't know you, and at first, they don't trust you and they are hoping to God you and 'Fido' know what you're doing."

Special operators like Clay are wired differently from most people. They love combat especially when Military Working Dogs are at their side. That's Clay in the photo on page 138 with his MWD and a pair of captured terrorists somewhere in the Middle East. His face has been deliberately obscured and his name changed because special operators can be called upon to work out of uniform in very hostile environments. Also, if bad guys in the US or elsewhere were to recognize him, he could be followed, putting him and his family in unnecessary danger.

When Clay was first offered an opportunity to work with the Breeding Program at Lackland, he saw the new job as an opportunity to protect troops in a new way. "Doc's training system is slow and steady and it works," Clay smiles as he leashes up a big-chested, one-year-old Malinois. As he gets the dog set for his next scheduled training scenario, Clay says Puppy School reminds him of the Green Beret's overseas training tasks. "In Special Forces, a very important part of our work is training people in their home countries who are usually enthusiastic about learning to shoot and fight but few of them come with reliable disciplines."

In those circumstances, he explains, the American special operator's job is to feel out each of the locals, get to know him, and find the best way into his head, past any cultural barriers to success. "Sometimes, you find yourself teaching fundamentals such as firing a rifle over and over again. You watch the way they use their eyes, the way their bodies move and then after they've missed the target yet again, after they've walked into the training ambush yet again, you find another way to get the lesson into their heads."

As he continues to describe the similarities between training foreign forces and American canines, Clay opens a door in the Breeding Program office and reveals a trove of leashes and training toys. He grabs a pair of thick, rubber Kong toys, one black, the other red. "Then one day," says Clay, "if we keep at it and do it right, every bit of our efforts just seem to click and instead of a very energized but unreliable, undisciplined yahoo, you've got a warrior you can probably count on to get the job done."

In his current job, Clay gets to help build future American Military Working Dogs who one day will go downrange in very bad places and alert on hidden dangers. If their handlers are paying attention, our troops will avoid IEDs and destroy ambushes that had been created to kill them.

Clay brings a dog into an environmental testing building. PHOTO BY LESLIE STONE-KAMEN.

"Unless I am totally wrong about this guy," says Clay as he gives yet another puppy a deep scratch, "he's going to graduate our Puppy School, make it through the Dog Training School to dual certify as an explosives detector and patrol Military Working Dog. One day, his first handler will be partnered to him and they will gradually become a team. It's a process that until you actually do it, you can never fully understand. So we just say, 'they begin to bond.'"

Clay says increasingly intense advanced training is supposed to inoculate the dog against most predictable combat shocks and is designed to keep the dog stable, even if his handler is killed or wounded so badly that the human can't continue to do his job.

On most missions downrange, outside the wire, once a MWD team leads the unit to hidden weapons, alerts on an IED, or reveals an ambush in the making, the dog's work is done. In the very next moment, gunfire and explosions can fill the air. If the terrorists see that their trap has been undone by the dog, the warrior pup and his handler become the enemy's priority target if they weren't already. Some terror groups offer cash bounties to their snipers to kill US handlers and dogs.

Whenever the circumstances permit, a handler rewards his furry partner with loud praise and a favorite toy, after the dog has alerted on an IED, an ambush, or a weapons cache. But of course a lot of that "paying" the warrior pup is delayed until the squad is fully out of harm's way. It must be emphasized that real-world combat is often laced with unpredictables and always offers the possibility of failure despite everyone's best efforts.

No matter how wonderful training has been, a lot can go wrong for a MWD and human partner. Clay explains that as a handler, "You keep in the back of your mind that Military Working Dogs—like human soldiers—can go into a kind of combat shock. Too many explosions, too much gunfire over too long a time and you've got a suddenly out-of-control war dog on your hands. The intensity of that stress can shut down the dog." In that awful moment, says Clay, "the dog can temporarily lose his training and even turn on your team." Clay says if you catch signs that your canine partner is melting down, "You do everything you can to get your dog out of there before he becomes a huge problem instead of an asset. You have to know what to do and then do it."

The MWD team is so valuable that the commander of the squad or team wants the dog and handler out of harm's way so he can use them the next time the unit goes back into combat. "In military terms," Clay says, "a properly trained dog is a true force-multiplier. He makes you a lot more effective in battle. He's out there to help us find the bad guys and bring us all home safe. I know of a handler who deliberately took a bullet for his MWD," Clay says, "and I understand it. I might even do it one day."

Two days later at Lackland, Clay is hooking a leash to the collar of a happy Belgian Malinois puppy. Like the other critters in Puppy School, this dog's previous encounters with Clay have taught him to expect a good time when the Special Ops guy shows up. Today the K9 is learning how to press his search even in an environment that's unstable.

The pup is watching Clay for his cue as to what game they're going to play next. Clay takes him into a two-story building. Inside are rooms in which piles of wood, clothing, mattresses, pillows, books, and plates are strewn all over. Following Clay's hand signals, the young dog jumps onto a table with a slippery surface that makes him stumble, but he balances himself and moves quickly,

This warrior pup's "dance" partner is Special Operator Clay J. PHOTO BY LESLIE STONE-KAMEN.

jumping down to the floor, seeking his target. He sniffs the area in front of him, moving in harmony with his handler. Suddenly, the warrior pup leaps up and paws at the top drawer of an old dresser. Inside, under a pile of clothing, is a bait that contains a small amount of the odor of a military grade explosive—a favorite among many terrorist bomb makers. "Good boy!" Clay calls out as he immediately produces a Kong toy, which the dog grabs with obvious pleasure.

That night, Clay is on the phone with another soldier stationed nearby deciding which civilian skydiving adventure they will share during the coming weekend. "We're like our dogs. We love the adrenaline," Clay laughs. 🐾

CHAPTER 25

THE PUPPY AND THE KNIFE

The knife that Air Force Colonel Tom S. carries was handed down to him. During World War II, Tom's grandfather was the first in his family to carry that blade into battle. Thirty years later, Tom's father wore it into combat in Vietnam. Today, Lackland's warrior pups are among the most potent weapons under Tom's coast-to-coast command.

He runs the USAF's 37th Training Group. That means he manages training components across the country, including the Dog Training School at Lackland and a Special Operations school more than a thousand miles away. Tom is an Air Force Academy graduate who also has three master's degrees. This scholar/warrior has a visceral connection to the heart of his mission, which is to prepare American warfighters for battle. He's been there himself with the family combat knife strapped down and his M9 pistol locked and loaded, directing airmen as they undertake anti-terrorist operations in Africa as well as Afghanistan.

Tom says there are lots of similarities in the personalities of the trainers at DTS and the instructors at the Special Operations school. "When you have individual units that have a specialized focus, and they train, day in

EVOLVING THREATS

"The world is constantly changing, threats are continually evolving, and our ability to counter those threats is vested in our ability to produce a quality product including MWDs and the handlers who love, train, and maintain them. That unit—handler and dog—is what is going to enhance our ability for force protection. I saw it happen again and again in Afghanistan," said Tom S.

Colonel Tom S. holds the combat knife passed down from his grandfather.
PHOTO BY JANET DELTUVA.

An MWD team searching for hidden explosives outside the US Air Force base in Bagram, Afghanistan, where Colonel Tom S. was responsible for security. PHOTO BY SENIOR AIRMAN CHRIS WILLIS.

and day out, from their initiation all the way to sustainment training, they realize that the mission they are committed to is highly important. Special operators and dog trainers and handlers gain a real sense of intense fidelity to their missions."

Tom thoroughly enjoys the remarkable, often larger-than-life characters in his command at DTS and Handlers' Course, where the men and women who partner with the dogs learn their life-saving trade. Tom sees what he describes as "a truly unique gamut, a kind of fine-tuning of personalities. And from there you start to find out who's got certain leadership skills that make them effective at being, say, a kennel master, and who's got certain leadership skills that make them effective at developing deployment strategy for the dogs." Tom says the challenge to commanders is to "make the best use of all this wonderful talent."

At an informal Thanksgiving supper for DTS instructors and their families at Lackland, Tom was the highest-ranking officer in the banquet room. He remained quietly in the background enjoying the scene as children played while their parents relaxed. At an awards ceremony a week earlier, two DTS instructors had been elevated to the prestigious pantheon of Red Patch master trainers. Both were women. Tom could barely hide his pride. "We look for capability—ability and aptitude," he explains. "Our career field [Air Force Security Forces, formerly Air Force Police] was gender-integrated in the 1970s and we have benefited from that rich history of women and men working together to accomplish the mission."

Tom was the commander of the 455th Expeditionary Security Forces squadron at Bagram Airfield in Afghanistan, "when the United States Air Force was responsible for controlling 220 square miles beyond the base perimeter or as our airmen say, 'outside the wire.'" Tom says his people reacted effectively under the maximum stress of combat and the subtle challenges of relationship building with local Afghans. "I saw that it didn't matter what the team's gender or racial composition was." Tom says his people were succeeding in all the challenge areas: village

EARNED TRUST

Colonel Tom S. is confident that all of the dogs who graduate the DTS at Lackland have the capability of becoming as effective as the dog who revealed the ambush that fateful day in Afghanistan. "The faith that our airmen, soldiers, marines and sailors have in our Military Working Dogs is phenomenal. There is a true sense of trust and it's been earned over and over again by our four-legged defenders, teamed with their brave two-legged handlers. It is an honor to serve with them."

engagement, observation, and partnership building. "In the midst of it, I saw a melding of Air Force family members into an expert team. It represented the faces of America. They came from all different backgrounds, from all genders and races. They came from different religious faiths and together what they realized was that the US Air Force family unit that they created in that squad is what became their power and their influence."

Tom spoke on the heels of yet another ISIS terror attack overseas, which murdered and wounded civilians. ISIS supporters had previously targeted military bases and recruiting stations inside the United States. "This latest outrage underlines the need for the protection that our defenders provide to our bases around the world and the value that our devoted canine friends teamed with well-trained handlers provide us. They multiply our force. To this date, we still do not have technology that is nearly as effective as the Military Working Dog."

Colonel Tom S. is her commanding officer, but in the moment this photo was taken, that little puppy commanded his heart. PHOTO COURTESY US DEFENSE DEPARTMENT.

WARRIOR PUPS

At Bagram and in the surrounding battle space, Tom relied on the skills and courage of the Military Working Dog teams assigned to his command. "Those MWD teams saved lives over and over again, detecting Taliban IEDs before our forces could come walk into those lethal traps."

With pain and anger, he remembers a case in which one of our airmen under his command fell in battle. "A courageous, Bagram-based Military Working Dog and his Security Forces handler detected a carefully planned Taliban ambush. The dog alerted and his handler shouted a warning." This saved the rest of the unit, but when the Taliban saw the dog had found them, they opened fire. "One of our people assigned as security overwatch to protect the MWD team saw the Taliban shooting and threw himself in the path of the bullets to protect the dog and handler," Tom says, his face etched with the memory. "The entire American squad was able to draw on its training and react with massive, focused gunfire, killing all of the enemy."

The single American loss in that engagement was the heroic overwatch defender. His sacrifice was critical to the survival of the rest of the squad including the K9 team. "Every American who survived and triumphed that day," says Tom, "will forever hold him in their hearts. As should we all." 🐾

MWD BBailey, a Breeding Program puppy, and his handler on guard at Bagram Airfield where Tom ran Security Forces before coming to Lackland.
PHOTO BY BOB HARRISON, US FORCES AFGHANISTAN.

CHAPTER 26

SERVICE BEFORE SELF

"Service Before Self" is the Air Force motto. The woman with the three Mals on the facing page lives this philosophy in retirement just as she did when she was a crucial team player on US Air Force surgical teams in Iraq, Germany, and the United States. Whether you're a dog or a person, Marie T. is the kind of person you want as a friend, neighbor, or colleague because she is good, kind, and always finds a way to get things done. When she enlisted, the US Air Force harnessed those qualities and trained her to be a surgical technician—the right job for someone with a compassionate heart, a quick mind, and able hands.

Like all who enlist, Marie entered the USAF through the Lackland gate. After Basic Military Training, which everyone must have, Air Force personnel experts read her aptitude tests, interviewed her, and set her on a career of caring for others.

When terrorists began using IEDs against our troops, thousands of our finest young men and women were rushed to America's top military hospital in Europe, the Landstuhl Regional Medical Center in

STANDARD OF CARE

Landstuhl is the Defense Department's largest and most advanced medical center outside the United States. When hostages are rescued from terrorists, when soldiers are wounded in combat, Landstuhl is often the first stop. The huge hospital is also close to the Army's renowned veterinary hospital called Dog Center Europe. In that facility, wounded and sick Military Working Dogs from Europe, the Middle East, Afghanistan, and Africa receive superb care.

Marie T. has fostered nine dogs and babysat dozens more from the DoD's Breeding Program. PHOTO BY JANET DELTUVA.

Kaiserslautern, Germany, home to more than fifty thousand US military and their families. Marie was there. Along with the rest of her surgical team she worked six or seven days a week, twelve to sixteen hours a day, most of that in the operating room, struggling to save the lives and limbs of American combat wounded from two ongoing wars.

If you've ever worked in an organization, you know there's always someone who becomes the go-to person when things are tough. That was Marie. Her bosses needed administrative help beyond the operating room and she rose to meet those needs as well. They kept heaping more responsibility on her and she kept getting it all done. Marie also wound up running the local chapter of Armed Forces Against Drunk Driving, a volunteer organization that gives free rides to military folks who've had too much to drink and know they need to be off the road, not behind the wheel.

Marie returned to Lackland twelve years after she first entered, to complete her Air Force career at the famed Wilford Hall Ambulatory Surgical Center. It was at Wilford Hall that she heard about the Military Working Dog Breeding Program's need for volunteer fosters to raise future MWDs. A chance to help people by loving and caring for puppies in her home? Perfect.

"When I first started fostering for the Department of Defense Military Working Dog Breeding Program," Marie says, "I never imagined that it would lead to where I am now. I thought I'd foster a couple puppies until the Air Force moved me to another duty station. I was so wrong. Six years later, I retired from active duty after fostering five and adopting two that had failed to meet all the training requirements. I adopted a third Mal after I retired."

In retirement, Marie wanted to stay connected to her Air Force brothers and sisters and to do what she could to help keep our troops safe. She also needed to work.

"I applied for, and was hired as an animal caretaker for all these magnificent dogs who I love as if they were my own." So Marie, who had given meticulous care to hundreds of human patients on three continents, now has a job—in a kennel.

Lackland's kennel, where Marie works, is meticulously maintained. PHOTO BY JANET DELTUVA.

However, the word *kennel* doesn't begin to describe the Lackland accommodations for visiting and resident canines. It's more like a kennel city with a support staff steeped in veterinary knowledge and the Lackland K9 spirit. There's room for more than eleven hundred dogs on the base and its neighboring Medina Annex.

That's a lot of barking, a whole lot of kibble, and tons of special diets, daily meds, exercise, and scheduled visits to the doctor to manage. It takes a highly disciplined, well-organized team. Marie was a natural fit for this unsung and mostly unseen crew whose outstanding work makes possible everything else at Lackland K9.

Marie says that the Lackland kennel crew is tasked with "safeguarding the health and welfare of all MWDs by observing, monitoring, and reporting any and all physical and emotional changes, regardless of the time of day or weather conditions." She sounds as if she's talking about taking care of her human patients. Of course, that's the point. 🐾

CHAPTER 27

JANET AND THE GOD OF WAR

Once you've had a deep friendship with a great dog and that dog passes from this life, you wonder if you will ever love like that again. That's how it was for Janet. Then, one day, she heard from a Lackland K9 caretaker about Ares, a young, patrol– and explosives detection–trained MWD. The handsome warrior pup had been diagnosed with a medical condition that made it impossible for him to live a life in the service. He needed adoption. Was Janet interested? Would she like to come to Lackland to meet him?

From the moment she saw him, her heart told her this was the one. He, however, was playing it cool and ignoring her. Janet slowly walked up to him and introduced herself. At first Ares allowed her to pet him lightly on his neck as she spoke soothingly to him. What came next cemented the deal. He made that rumbling sound of canine satisfaction. He's named after the ancient Greek god of war. The time had come for this seasoned warrior to stand down. Like a story with a great ending, Ares was about to retire to his new and forever home with another American warrior, Colonel Janet Deltuva, who, until she retired, was the deputy command surgeon of the Air Force Global Strike Command.

During her career, Janet served at US Air Force bases at home and around the world, including the strategic US base in Kunsan, South Korea and at the legendary Andrews Air Force Base outside Washington, DC, which is home to Air Force One. By the time she assumed her responsibilities as the number two boss at Andrews Medical Center, she had already come to love US Military Working Dogs and kept a supply of dog cookies at her desk.

"Large cargo planes arrived at our flight line three times a week," she remembers. "Those planes brought us wounded, ill, and injured service members from Landstuhl Army Regional Medical Center in Germany." As those planes landed, part of Janet's job was to oversee the quality of care. "Some of the human patients arriving at Andrews would go on to Walter Reed

That's Colonel Janet Deltuva, USAF-Retired, with former MWD Ares. Today, he's her house pet, but he's always got her back. PHOTO BY JACQUELYN SMELTER.

Janet first met MWD Emzy at the US Air Force base in Kunsan, South Korea. USAF PHOTO/STAFF SGT. JONATHAN POMEROY.

Army Hospital or Bethesda Naval Medical Center; others would remain in our Aeromedical Staging Facility awaiting transport to other, specialized hospitals and treatment centers," Janet says. Some of these treatments last for months and even years in the cases that included extreme burns, lost limbs, traumatic brain injuries, and PTSD.

To make them feel welcome and fully supported as they await the transport to their next phase of their care, all human patients on those flights are met and escorted off the aircraft by members of their own military service and specialty. Our military treats MWDs with the same respect as human warfighters. As a result, when K9 patients arrive from one of these flights, they are met by people who immediately understand their needs—MWD handlers.

"Sometimes, the dogs are what we call 'walkie-talkies'—recovered enough to walk around on the plane and visit other passengers after the aircraft lands. These dogs—and this is without special training—go to work immediately as therapy dogs. It is as though they have been handed a pamphlet on how to be a morale booster with wounded humans. They just know what to do," Janet recalls with a warm smile.

It is sweet to watch the men and women patients awaiting transport light up whenever a dog walks into their space. Medical staff aboard the plane heard a lot of, "Here, boy!" and "Good dog!" as the walkie-talkie warrior pups went from stretcher to stretcher, seat to seat, and spread their canine good vibes among the human heroes.

In the cases of MWDs staying overnight at Andrews, Janet welcomed the handlers who came to accompany the dogs to stay. Regularly, "The handlers volunteered to sleep in the kennels with the dog, because as one of them told her, 'that will make the dog more comfortable.'"

The military doesn't do all these kind and respectful things to get great press coverage. Nobody even tells the press. "We do it," Janet says, "because we truly love and respect our four-legged battle buddies. They are our brothers and sisters in the fight and we honor them exactly as such."

MWD team guarding an F-16 at Kunsan Air Base in South Korea, where Janet ran the base hospital. PHOTO BY SENIOR AIRMAN COLEVILLE MCFEE.

After Janet's assignment at Andrews was completed, she was assigned to South Korea to be commander of the hospital at the strategic US Air Force base at Kunsan only fifteen minutes by fighter jet to the North Korean border. She kept encountering Emzy, an especially sweet four-legged defender of the base.

A few months before Janet's Kunsan deployment ended, she learned that MWD Emzy, age eight, had been diagnosed with an irregular heartbeat—a condition that was forcing her into early retirement after six years of keeping the base safe. Colonel Deltuva asked to adopt Emzy. Of course, this was no civilian dog adoption.

Janet's graceful photos of the puppies and people of Lackland K9 capture the love felt in the community. Here, a foster mom and her son visit the MWD National Monument with their pup—a Lackland tradition. PHOTO BY JANET DELTUVA.

Emzy could not leave the Air Force without special training that essentially undid a lot of what she had learned at the beginning of her career. Like police K9s and all MWDs certified in patrol, Emzy had been taught to intimidate, to attack on command, and to intervene in violence near her, even if her handler was not under threat. While appropriate skills for a war dog, they are not acceptable for a US MWD no longer in service. The reset training worked, and Emzy followed Janet to her next assignment, and into retirement. Emzy shared five years of love and fun with Janet and her husband.

Emzy passed at age thirteen after a brave fight with various illnesses associated with canine old age. Throughout her care, the very expensive prescription veterinary medications Emzy needed were provided free of charge by the non-governmental US War Dogs Association Foundation. More than 375 retired American war dogs now receive free medication through the foundation created by a former handler.

MEET ARES'S MOM

Janet Deltuva, contributing photographer and technical advisor on this book, is an American hero (though she would deny it). She was working at the Pentagon on September 11, 2001 when terrorists flew a hijacked airliner into the huge building, killing 184 people. Within seconds of the attack, Janet raced to the scene and helped with the medical response.

Janet was still mourning Emzy when she got that invitation to meet Ares at Lackland. Lucky dog. Blessed Janet. She has the love of another great dog in her life. ❧

CHAPTER 28

CHERISHED

We all love our dogs. But the bond between Military Working Dogs and their handlers is in a class by itself. Here are two true tales of MWDs who have been particularly cherished by the human warriors with whom they served.

US Marine Corps explosives detection dog Lucca is the first American war dog to receive the Dickin Medal, the world's top award for canine heroism, for her four hundred combat patrols which resulted in finding dozens of IEDs that otherwise would have killed hundreds of men and women.

On her final patrol in Afghanistan, Lucca detected her fortieth hidden bomb, saving yet another patrol of US Marines from destruction. Then it happened. According to the Dickin Medal report, "Cpl. (Juan M.) Rodriguez sent Lucca to clear a nearby path when a 30 pound pressure plate IED detonated underneath her," sending her flying and doing major damage to her body. Instantly, Corporal Rodriguez's training clicked in.

MWD Lucca and her last handler, Corporal Juan M. Rodriguez. PHOTO BY CORPORAL JENNIFER PIRANTE USMC.

Handlers cover the body of MWD Breston with the American flag.
PHOTO BY AIRMAN 1ST CLASS KIANA BROTHERS.

"Mamma" Lucca, America's most successful MWD, poses for her portrait. PHOTO BY CORPORAL JENNIFER PIRANTE USMC.

God summoned the beast from the field and He said
"Behold, man is created in my image. Therefore, adore him.
Protect him
Guide him through the perils along the way
This shall be your destiny and your immortality."
So spoke the Lord
And the dog heard, and was content
—from "God Summoned a Beast" (author unknown)

Lucca runs on her three legs. PHOTO BY CORPORAL JENNIFER PIRANTE USMC.

"The explosion was huge and I immediately feared the worst for Lucca," Corporal Rodriguez said. "I ran to her and saw her struggling to get up. I picked her up and ran to the shelter of a nearby tree line, applied a tourniquet to her injured leg and called the medics to collect us. I stayed with her constantly throughout her operation and her recovery. She had saved my life on so many occasions. I had to make sure that I was there for her when she needed me."

As Lucca has come to symbolize the potential power of each MWD, Rodriguez's actions in the field and afterward have come to demonstrate the superbly trained first aid skills and pure, unselfish love and courage that handlers share with their canine partners.

Sometimes that love can be seen with great clarity while handler and dog are alive and well. But it is also visible surrounding the death of any dog while still in service, such as MWD Breston.

MWD Breston jumps for joy with chew toy.
PHOTO BY AIRMAN 1ST CLASS KIANA BROTHERS.

After he graduated the Dog Training School at Lackland, Breston was sent to his permanent home base at the 375th Security Forces Squadron, Scott Air Force Base in Illinois where he served and from where he deployed to Afghanistan. For almost eight and a half years this tough, smart, spirited, patrol detection dog lived a life of adventure protecting our troops.

During his career Breston had a staggering thirteen consecutive handlers. He made his huge heart available to each and every one of them. The aging war dog was about to retire when a watchful veterinarian at Scott discovered that Breston had an incurable cancer that was already causing him severe pain, which was sure to get a lot worse. Some of his Security Forces pals wanted to give him a last meal. They surprised Breston with a juicy steak. Had he been his healthy self, that steak would have made him very happy. But the big MWD was too weak from the cancer. His utter disinterest in the steak signaled the imminent end of Breston's watch. The decision was made to protect Breston from the escalating pain by euthanizing him.

Later that same day, Breston's final handler, Air Force Staff Sergeant David Y., stroked Breston's face and spoke gently to him. The dog knew he was not alone. His beloved partner was right there with him, as

Farewell—Breston's kiss goodbye. PHOTO BY AIRMAN 1ST CLASS KIANA BROTHERS.

the veterinarian injected the chemicals that painlessly ended the dog's suffering. As Breston's last breath left his body, David leaned in and kissed Breston's head.

"Breston was a beast," said David. "He loved to work. He was very protective of me. I felt a tremendous amount of sadness seeing him pass away. Breston meant the world to me. The bond between us was very strong."

A memorial service with full military honors was held in memory of Breston, who had deployed to a war zone to protect US soldiers and survived the many threats there, only to have cancer end his life of devoted service to his handler and his country.

TAPS

Being a MWD handler is not only a high-risk job, it is the embodiment of so much of what is beautiful and inspiring about being human.

In every major building in K9 country at Lackland, there is a wall of honor with twenty-three plaques. Each plaque is about the size of a family bible and bears the photograph of a young man or woman who fell in battle. Each was a great American warrior with a heart of courage as big as the universe itself. These men and women were killed in Iraq and Afghanistan as they led the way for their units while watching for cues that their canine partners had found hidden IEDs or detected enemy ambushes. That capability made them priority targets for the enemy. Each fallen handler is an American hero, a national treasure.

Between September 11, 2001 and the day this book went to press, an estimated sixty American military working dogs and twenty-three handlers had been killed in action. We hold all of them in our hearts. Every dog who completes training at Lackland has the same mission: to protect our troops even at the cost of their own lives. They share that mission and that risk with their human partners. If only we all had that kind of bravery.

As handlers say with pride, "K9 leads the way!" 🐾

RESOURCES

ORGANIZATIONS THAT PROVIDE SERVICES FOR HANDLERS AND MWDS

Military Working Dog Team Support Association. Inc. (mwdtsa.org)

MWDTSA's mission is to support current and retired deployed Military Working Dog Teams, veteran dog handler events and causes, war dog memorials, and educational opportunities.

Mission K9 Rescue (missionk9rescue.org)

Mission K9 Rescue is dedicated to "rescue, reunite, re-home, rehabilitate, and repair" any retired working dog that has served mankind in some capacity.

Support Police K9s, ProjectPawsAlive (projectpawsalive.org)

Project Paws Alive is dedicated to providing customized ballistic stab and bullet-protective K9 vests, K9 first aid field trauma kits, K9 cooling vest, K9 vehicle heat alarms and other vital K9 equipment to law enforcement, fire, search and rescue, and military K9s throughout the US who cannot otherwise afford this equipment.

US War Dog Association (uswardogs.org)

Dedicated to former and current Military Dog Handlers and supporting members committed to promoting the long history of Military Service Dogs, establishing permanent war dog memorials and educating the public about the invaluable services and sacrifice of these canines to our country. They assist in the process of adopting retiring military and police canines. They established "Operation Military Care K9" that sends care packages to Military Working Dog Teams (handlers and K9s) overseas.

NON-PROFIT ORGANIZATIONS THAT PROVIDE SERVICE DOGS FOR VETERANS

Alpha K9 (alphak9.org)

Always Faithful Dogs (alwaysfaithfuldogs.org)

America's VetDogs (vetdogs.org)

American Humane Association (americanhumane.org)

Assistance Service Dog Educational Center (servicedogcenter.org)

Canine Companions for Independence (cci.org)

Canines with a Cause (canineswithacause.com)

Freedom Dogs (freedomdogs.org)

Freedom Service Dogs of America (freedomservicedogs.org)

Hawaii Fi-Do (hawaiifido.org)

K9s for Warriors (k9sforwarriors.org)

New Horizons Service Dogs (newhorizonsservicedogs.org)

Patriot PAWS Service Dogs (patriotpaws.org)

Paws for Purple Hearts (pawsforpurplehearts.org)

Sam Simon Foundation (samsimonfoundation.com)

Save-A-Vet (save-a-vet.org)

Service Dog Project, Inc. (servicedogproject.org)

A Veteran's Best Friend (servicedog4ptsd.org)

Warrior Canine Connection (warriorcanineconnection.org)

PHOTOS BY JANET DELITUVA.

SPECIAL THANKS

Leslie and I wish to thank the dozens of other Lackland K9 folks who helped us create this book. Although there is space for only eight photos, we offer our humble gratitude to all.

Brandon, who lets his foster know he has his back. PHOTO BY LORA HARRIST.

Sarah, who babies her fosters. PHOTO BY JEFF KAMEN.

DTS trainer Dontay, whose special power is kindness. PHOTO BY JEFF KAMEN.

DTS trainer Jake, who shows gentle self-confidence to warrior pups. PHOTO BY JEFF KAMEN

David, who's devoted to his foster pup. PHOTO BY JANET DELTUVA.

Wick, a Handlers Course instructor, reunited with his foster. FAMILY PHOTO.

Beth (right), who fostered baby QQuantico. FAMILY PHOTO.

Pete (right), observing his new foster pup with a trainer. FAMILY PHOTO.